hamlyn

Teach your child to

Sleep

Solving sleep problems
from newborn
through childhood

Millpond
bringing harmony

First published in
Great Britain in 2005 by
Hamlyn, a division of Octopus
Publishing Group Ltd
2-4 Heron Quays, London E14 4JP

Distributed in the United States
and Canada by
Sterling Publishing Co., Inc.
387 Park Avenue South, New York,
NY 10016-8810

ISBN 0 600 61345 3
EAN 9780600613459

A CIP catalogue record for this book
is available from the British Library

Printed and bound in China

10 9 8 7 6 5 4 3 2 1

Contents

The Millpond Children's Sleep Clinic approach

There is one topic that probably preoccupies the parents of babies and young children more than any other: sleep, and how to get more of it.

The monopoly that this has on parents' conversations implies that sleep problems in babies and young children are inevitable, that they are very difficult to solve, that children will eventually grow out of them, and that, meanwhile, you just have to endure it. We have seen hundreds of families who have struggled on with this debilitating belief. We have also seen them come out of it. But they all needed help.

Sleep problems are, paradoxically, often complex in their nature but, at the same time, relatively simple to deal with. They are complex because they can be deeply engrained and multi-faceted. But they are simple because, once you have isolated the nature of the problem, there is a small but well-defined battery of techniques with which to confront them.

The techniques we use at Millpond Children's Sleep Clinic are not new or unique to us. They are well-recognized core techniques that have been fully researched and used by many professionals around the world.

What distinguishes our approach is that we do not adhere to any one of these techniques in a given situation. Families are not laboratories in which to test scientifically proven sleep strategies. We believe that the solution to a sleep problem must take into account the particular family's environment, composition, needs and expectations. So we take a tailor-made approach: one that is sympathetic rather than prescriptive and that always has the child at its centre.

All the techniques recommended in this book have been tried and tested at Millpond. They have worked for hundreds of children – and their exhausted parents – and we hope that, through this book, they will work for many more.

Although we have 15 years of experience with children's sleep problems between us, we are not just health professionals with an academic or clinical knowledge of sleep disorders. As mothers ourselves, we have been through the problems that you are experiencing with our own children. So we know just how difficult it can be emotionally to deal with the problems hands on. We also know that, with clear direction shaped to the individual family's needs, you can teach your child to sleep.

We aim to guide you through the practical options so that you can choose the right solution for you and adapt it to your family's needs. Our experience tells us that, from that point onwards, you are only 2–3 weeks from having a baby or child who knows how to sleep – and enjoys it. However, we hope that, on the way, you will have learned enough to tackle other sleep problems that may occur, with this child or your next.

The name of our clinic was chosen to reflect the transition from chaos to calm that comes with teaching your child to sleep well. We hope that, with the guidance in this book, we can help you make that transition.

Mandy Gurney and Tracey Marshall

There is a direct relation between sleeping properly and performing well during the day.

How to use this book

This book is designed to help you to understand the nature of the sleep problem that you and your child are experiencing, and to identify an appropriate solution. Knowing exactly why, when and how your child should sleep, and sharing in the experiences of other parents, will help you move towards practical solutions.

You can use this book in a number of ways. Reading chapter by chapter will give you an overall view of basic sleep patterns and needs, followed by practical solutions for dealing with problems. Those wishing to tackle specific problems can turn to the practical chapters first and return to the theory later.

Chapter by chapter

The book describes what sleep is all about and how it develops as a child grows from birth. It explains how parents can encourage good sleep habits and identify sleep problems as they arise. Perhaps most importantly, it gives practical advice on techniques to solve sleep problems, and step-by-step methods for identifying how best to tackle your own child's sleep problems.

Key problems

Many parents will have bought this book because they are experiencing specific sleep problems with a child and wish to find a solution.

Chapter by chapter

Chapter 1 Examines the basics of sleep, for example, why children need sleep, how their sleep patterns change and how their normal development influences their sleep. A little knowledge of the science of sleep will give you a head start in treating your problem effectively.

Chapter 2 Looks at how good sleep habits are formed, and how you can adapt your circumstances both to encourage them and to avoid the conditions that contribute to sleep problems.

Chapter 3 Looks at the types and causes of the wide range of sleep problems – some common, some rare – that we deal with as clinicians at the Millpond Children's Sleep Clinic.

Chapter 4 Describes the various techniques that can be applied in solving children's sleep problems. This will guide you in choosing the right solution for your child.

Chapter 5 Sets out a series of flow charts that explore different variations of common problems.

Chapter 6 Describes the programmes implemented by real families that we have advised over the past 10 years. The experiences of these families are both instructive and encouraging, and you will see how the principles outlined earlier in the book have been successfully applied.

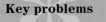
Key problems

If adhered to, a sleep programme should bring the desired results within a month.

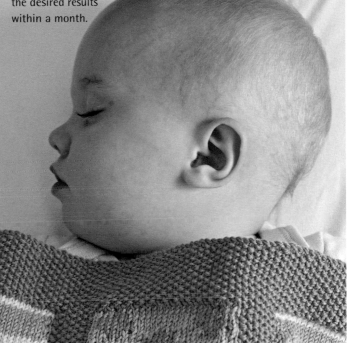

Turn to Chapter 3 for common sleep problems.

If you want to know if you are encouraging good sleep habits, turn to the dos and don'ts on page 48.

If you believe that you know the cause of your child's sleep problem, but need help in assessing your situation, look at the 10 key questions on page 70.

Turn to Chapter 4 for sleep-training techniques.

If you are experiencing problems applying a sleep-training technique, look at the What if...? pages 84–89.

Turn to Chapter 5 for flow charts that will help you to tailor a programme to suit your particular family situation.

If you want to read about real life situations, and how they were overcome, read through the case studies in Chapter 6.

If this is the case, turning to specific practical sections of this book will help to show that no problem is insurmountable, and that there are simple steps that you can take to overcome them.

Please recognize that the advice contained in this book is for otherwise healthy children. If your child has an underlying medical problem, you will almost certainly need to address this first. Similarly, if your child is currently unwell, you may be advised to wait until he is fully recovered before using these techniques to solve sleep problems.

Identifying your priorities

How and why do you want to teach your child to sleep? It may seem an odd question, but people have different motives for wanting their children to sleep better and different hopes for the outcome.

Some parents want their baby to sleep through the night as soon as possible come what may, so that their own life is minimally disrupted. Others are happy to let time be their guide, allowing their baby's spontaneous sleep patterns to set the agenda.

Take time to decide where you are on this spectrum and talk to your partner about it. This will enable you to be realistic about what is possible and what is practical for you and your family, and to establish how far you are willing to compromise on your ideals and expectations and how strong your commitment is.

Realistic goals are easier to meet and impose less stress on you as parents and on your child. Realistic expectations will save you from the guilt trap into which many parents fall when their well-laid plans are brought to a halt by the chaos of daily family life.

If you are currently unsure about your hopes and expectations, answering the questions (see Box below) should help you to focus and orientate yourself.

What kind of parent are you?

There are a range of techniques for dealing with sleep problems (see Chapter 4) and it is unlikely that all of them will suit every parent. Some parents may be disciplinarians, others more lenient; some are anxious about their child's progress, others more relaxed. Naturally the child is your main focus and his needs are at the heart of this, but it is also important to consider your own attitudes to life – and your own limitations.

The sleep programme that you choose is more likely to work if it has some compatibility with your parenting style. This also applies to getting agreement

---

Questions to ask yourself

Before you embark on a sleep plan, answer the following questions.

- Does my child really have a sleep problem? (If you are unsure, see page 16, What is normal sleep?)

- Do my partner and I agree that something needs to be done about it?

- Do we have the will and energy right now to start a sleep programme and to engage in the process for 3 weeks if necessary?

- Where can we call on outside support if things get difficult?

- Is my child old enough to be involved in discussing the plan?

- Will my child be able to cope with a highly disciplined plan of action?

For a more detailed assessment, see page 70, Assessing your child's problem.

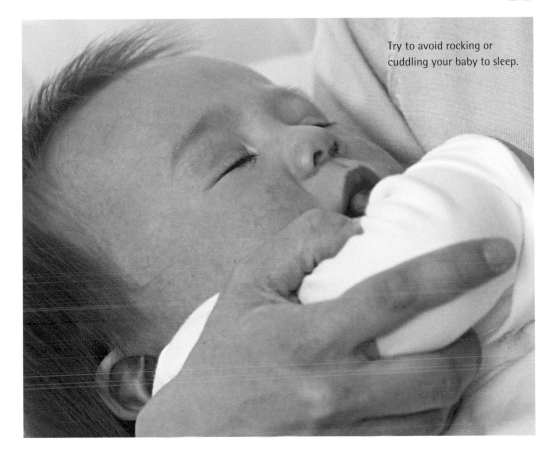

Try to avoid rocking or cuddling your baby to sleep.

between you and your partner, as a sleep problem shared is a sleep problem partly solved. Whether one or both of you are on the case, and whether or not you have similar parenting styles, consistency is a golden rule that together you need to make an effort not to break.

The child's point of view

In examining the different strategies open to you, and the domestic environment in which they will operate, it is important not to lose sight of the most important component: your child. Although he needs to operate within your particular family environment, he is an individual with his own tendencies and preferences.

A child's temperament should not dictate what you decide to do but it will influence your decision. As parents, you may feel that some techniques are not appropriate for your child. If you have a very sensitive child, for example, a technique that confers a sense of isolation or exclusion may not work well in practice.

This is important to remember if you are also dealing with the sleep problems of a second or subsequent child: he may not be like his older brother or sister and may require different handling.

Lastly, if you have identified a new solution or found an effective method in the past, remember that children change! What worked at 4 months of age is unlikely to work in the same way if the problem recurs at 12 months. You may need to adjust your tactics and certainly your expectations.

Child-carers can help

If your child is being cared for by someone else during the day, you need to consider the other people involved.

It pays to involve a young child's carers in your plans so that they share the responsibility for implementing them effectively in the hours when you are not around. Reminding other carers that they will also reap the benefits of a better behaved child at the end may be useful!

1 Understanding sleep

The importance of sleep

Thanks to extensive scientific investigations, we now know what happens to the brain and body at different stages of sleep. There are still some unanswered questions, and strangely one of those is why we need sleep in the first place.

However, what we do know from everyday experience is that we cannot do without it. Sleep is a vital function and it affects our physical and mental performance profoundly. A good night's sleep leaves us refreshed, alert and confident to face the challenges of the day ahead. Conversely, a bad night's sleep deprives us of the concentration, energy and ability to do the things we need to in everyday life. And as parents, for most of us that is a lot of things.

The effect on babies and children is even more profound (see Boxes). Insufficient sleep compromises their vital ability to learn, relax and even grow. Recent studies have shown that learning to sleep better improves children's appetites, lifts their mood and enhances their intellectual ability.

More sleep means brighter children

Anyone who has had to rouse a baby or child from deep slumber before they have rested adequately is familiar with the adverse effects. Babies often react by being restless, grizzly and difficult to settle; they may demand feeding for comfort, falling asleep on the rebound then waking half an hour later, still in a restless state. In toddlers, lack of sleep often leads to impatience, poor appetite, clinginess and tempera-mental behaviour. This can have a snowball effect because, paradoxically, the over-tired baby or child finds it more difficult to sleep.

When this is repeated over time, it has a compound effect that can interfere with the child's learning and development. Although this starts to become apparent in the early years, it can show up most when the child starts school. A recent study of schoolchildren by the American Sleep Foundation demonstrated a direct link between shortage of sleep and poor performance in the classroom. It estimated that many children are missing out on 2 hours sleep a night.

The good news is that learning to sleep well improves children's mood, behaviour and performance dramatically and quickly. Their mood is often demon-strably elevated, making them easier to care for at every age, both inside and outside the home. Schoolteachers have reported that, when children get

---

Why young brains need sleep

The sleeping brain is not a resting brain, but works to make sense of what children have seen and learned in their waking hours. Dreaming sleep, or rapid eye movement (REM) sleep (see page 18) benefits children's learning by increasing the blood supply to the brain, with the following results.

- They become more alert mentally.

- Their ability to retain information is optimized.

- Their senses are sharpened and cognitive ability is enhanced.

- Their brain can better process information.

Why young bodies need sleep

When babies and children sleep, they spend more time than adults in slow-wave, non-REM sleep (see page 18). This is when the body restores itself, carrying out several essential tasks.

- More blood is directed to the developing muscles.

- Growing tissues are repaired as cells divide more quickly.

- Vital hormones are released for growth and development.

- White blood cells are produced, which support the immune system.

more sleep, they show improved concentration and application in the classroom and are more likely to enjoy and fit in with their school environment.

Your sleep matters too

The effect of sleep deprivation is not restricted to your children. The irregular sleep patterns of a baby or toddler who has not yet learned to sleep predictably also deprive parents of the sleep that they need too. Being on call for restless infants, especially during the night, can leave you feeling as if you have interminable jet-lag, without the holiday photographs for comfort.

Perhaps one of your reasons for wanting to teach your child to sleep is that you will be able to sleep better. Don't dismiss this as being selfish. If you are more rested, you will feel better equipped to handle your child. Your confidence as a parent will increase, and a more confident parent results in a happier child.

We have found that the effect can go much further. Solving a baby's or child's sleep problem can lift the spirit of the whole family.

Sleeping for life

A child who learns to sleep well in his early years not only reaps immediate psychological and physical rewards but also learns habits that will benefit him for life. Psychologists have shown that people who had poor sleep habits as children are more susceptible to sleep problems, such as insomnia, in adult life. These can naturally interfere with an individual's ambitions and achievements. Some people can survive, and even thrive, on very little sleep, but they are rare exceptions.

Teaching children to sleep well does not just benefit the parents who are caring for them. It also sets up habits that will help sustain them through the changing challenges and pressures of their teenage and adult years, when the energy and clarity of a rested mind and body give them the resources they need. Sleeping well is about more than good conduct or conformity. It is about laying the essential foundations for a healthy life.

A good night's sleep will increase daytime energy levels.

What is normal sleep?

As with any other aspect of their daily lives, individual children differ in the way that they sleep, just as they differ in the way that they play, eat or talk. However, the general progression in the way their sleep develops is common to almost all children.

In the early weeks and months, young babies have completely different sleep phases and schedules to us, as well as generally unpredictable sleep habits. It helps to be aware of this difference, so that you know what to expect and when to intervene if the pattern seems abnormal.

However, by the age of 4 years, the vast majority of children adopt what we might consider an adult pattern of sleep. The only big difference is the quantity they need. Although individual children differ in this respect too, most need a recommended minimum for optimum health.

1–3 months

The expression 'to sleep like a baby' is well chosen. In the early weeks of life, babies sleep for an average of 16 hours out of every 24. This is divided equally between day and night. Life for parents would be very simple if this came in one big chunk, but of course it is split into many periods of 2–4 hours, which are scattered throughout your own sleeping and waking times.

This unpredictable pattern is due to the slow development of the biological clock (see Box), which means that new babies cannot distinguish night from day. Rather than taking light or darkness as their cues, during these first few weeks they rely more on their tummies, and wake and sleep accordingly depending on whether they feel hungry or sated, respectively.

Most babies can distinguish night from day by the age of 10 weeks, a stage of development that parents greet with great relief. As their daytime naps drop from about four to three by the end of the third month, they sleep for longer periods at night. In fact, three-quarters of all babies are sleeping for a large unbroken period during the night by 3 months.

3–6 months

This is a period of rapid change, with the amount of sleep babies require dropping to about 14 hours. Although this change is driven by the baby's biological development, it is also a period in which parents can strongly influence when this sleep occurs, to their own and their baby's mutual advantage. This is because, by 3–4 months, babies are not only biologically ready to sleep through the night but also increasingly responsive to routines set by their parents. It is probably an early window of opportunity for sleep training that should not be missed.

6–12 months

Over this period there is a distinct shift in the balance of night-time and daytime sleep, and by 9 months most babies need just one morning and one afternoon nap. Both this and the length of night-time sleep become more predictable, enabling parents to plan activities around the baby and, just as importantly, to get more regular, unbroken sleep themselves.

Biological time-keeping

The body clock is the main sleep/wake regulator. It governs the release and timing of most mood, energy and sleep-related hormones. The body clock uses signals like sunlight and darkness to know when to produce and shut down sleep hormones. The clock cycles through these hormones about every 24 to 25 hours, known as circadian rhythm. Lack of a sleep/wake routine will throw off our body clocks.

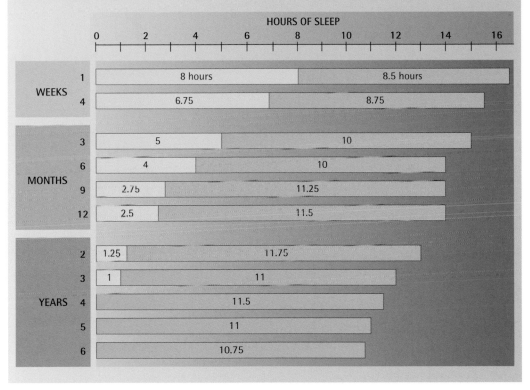

Average sleep needs in childhood

Most children develop along the same lines when it comes to the amount of day- and night-time sleep they need as they grow older. Generally, daytime sleep decreases as night-time increases.

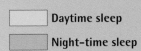

Daytime sleep

Night-time sleep

HOURS OF SLEEP

		Daytime	Night-time
WEEKS	1	8 hours	8.5 hours
	4	6.75	8.75
MONTHS	3	5	10
	6	4	10
	9	2.75	11.25
	12	2.5	11.5
YEARS	2	1.25	11.75
	3	1	11
	4		11.5
	5		11
	6		10.75

1–3 years

At some point over the middle of this period, it is normal for most babies to shift their morning nap forwards to around lunchtime. This nap typically lasts 1½–2 hours and means that they can subsequently drop their afternoon nap.

Towards the age of 3 years, the length of this nap will decrease again, to about an hour. This is complemented by an 11-hour sleep at night, which often makes parents' lives easier. Good sleeping habits can easily be disrupted during this period: the circadian rhythm is still developing and can be easily upset by a holiday, illness, or a change in sleeping arrangements, so it is important to adhere to a good bedtime routine.

3–6 years

By the middle of this period, circadian rhythms are fully established. As long as children are sleeping well at night, they will drop daytime naps altogether. However, their adoption of a mature sleeping pattern is not accompanied by a significant reduction in the amount of sleep that they need. This is worth remembering because a shortage of sleep will still affect their behaviour.

Sleep cycles

Sleep is not a single state and is not, as is commonly supposed, simply the opposite of 'awake'. A normal night's sleep is made up of several identifiable sleep cycles, which we can consciously distinguish and which have different biological functions.

This applies to people of any age, but the cycles occur in different quantities and at different times in babies and young children. Knowing when and why they occur helps you to understand your child's sleep patterns. This in turn helps you to determine whether they are indicative of a sleep problem or simply a reflection of these natural cycles.

Types of sleep

Scientists categorize sleep into five main stages, passing from drowsiness down through light and dream sleep into increasingly deeper sleep. One of the principal distinctions, which is useful for parents to know, is that between the light phase of sleep, known as rapid eye movement (REM), and deeper non-rapid eye movement (non-REM) sleep.

REM sleep Rapid eye movement sleep is the state in which we dream. It is the first sleep state to develop, appearing in the baby in the womb at about 6 months' gestation, and it is vital to the development of a baby's brain. During REM sleep, the body switches off and the brain receives extra blood and warms up, indicating a greater level of activity. This is probably when a baby's brain processes what she has sensed during her waking hours.

Because of its developmental importance, babies spend a lot of time in REM sleep. At birth it accounts for 50 per cent of their sleep, falling gradually to around 33 per cent by the age of 3 years. From later childhood and into adulthood, it makes up 25 per cent of sleep.

Parents of toddlers will have noticed that, from the age of about 2 years, most children are aware of their dreams, which can be very vivid, and start to talk about them. You can see it in action for yourself. Most children twitch occasionally in their sleep, move their eyeballs back and forth under their eyelids, and breathe irregularly when they dream.

The proportion of REM sleep increases as the night goes on, with most therefore coming in the early hours of the morning. As REM sleep is mentally restorative, this explains why someone who is woken up too early will often be mentally 'foggy' for the rest of the day. This applies to adults as much as children (see page 66, Looking after yourself).

Non-REM sleep During this state of slow-wave sleep, your child will lie quietly, her muscles relaxed. She will breathe steadily and deeply and remain motionless. This is the condition that most people think of as sleep, but non-REM has not developed fully until a baby is 4 months old.

Non-REM is to the body what REM is to the brain. It is the time when blood is released to the muscles, tissue is grown or repaired and hormones are released for growth and development.

What sleep cycles mean for your child

The sleep cycle in a full-term newborn baby is about 50–60 minutes long, but increases at around 3 months of age to about 90 minutes, a pattern that is then maintained for life. Whichever the length of the cycle, it is in the lighter moments of sleep between cycles that your child is most likely to rouse. You may see her stir at this point, often moving or muttering, but if left undisturbed she should go back to sleep.

A newborn will enter the REM state as soon as she falls asleep, while an older baby or child will go into non-REM sleep first. It takes up to 15 minutes for a baby to fall asleep fully, although most children should do so more quickly. Once asleep, it takes about 10 minutes to enter deep sleep and waking your child from this stage of sleep may be almost impossible. This is very relevant when applying a sleep-training technique (see page 74, Sleep-training techniques).

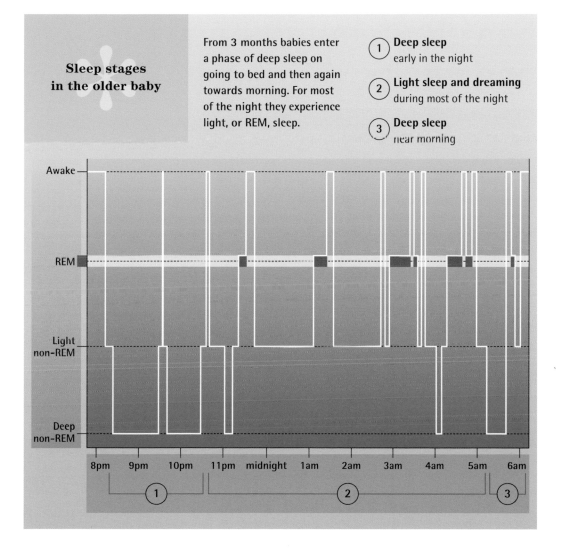

Sleep stages in the older baby

From 3 months babies enter a phase of deep sleep on going to bed and then again towards morning. For most of the night they experience light, or REM, sleep.

1 **Deep sleep** early in the night

2 **Light sleep and dreaming** during most of the night

3 **Deep sleep** near morning

Taking longer than 20 minutes may indicate a problem, such as late naps (see page 32) or inappropriate sleep associations (see page 53).

If you are putting your child to bed around 7.30–8.00 pm, her first sleep cycle will end at around 9–9.30 pm and her second at around 10.30–11.00 pm. This is the time when many parents go to bed and they often assume that it is the noise they make that disturbs their child. It is more likely that the child will rouse anyway, so although keeping the disturbance to a minimum is obviously helpful, there is no need to be over-cautious.

Unfortunately, adult sleep cycles do not coincide with those of children, so your child may often rouse when you are in deep sleep. This is quite likely to happen after 2.00 am, when your child's REM sleep increases. There is little you can do about this, except share the visits to your child – when they are necessary – with your partner.

Developmental stages and sleep

If the pattern of your child's life didn't change from one week to the next and all you had to do was teach him to sleep, it would be easy. But, of course, babies and children change all the time. These developments can interfere with the process of learning to sleep. Sometimes, however, they also help speed it up. Anticipating these changes and their impact can make it easier to adapt to them.

0–6 months

This is the period of most rapid development in babies and it is also the period during which they sleep most. Inevitably, the accelerated biological and environmental changes they experience when awake have a strong impact on their sleep.

When babies are born they are unable to distinguish night from day. Although they will have sensed the difference between night and day in the womb from the movement or stillness of their mother, they cannot at first connect this with light and dark.

However, it takes only a week or two for them to start making the connection. This does not mean they will sleep whenever it is dark. But it is the very beginning of an awareness which, if reinforced by you, will enable them to start doing so within just a few weeks of being born.

Babies can distinguish between night and day by 6–8 weeks.

Their sleeping and waking patterns are influenced as much by hunger as by the circadian rhythms around them. They tend to wake when hungry and very often fall asleep straight after feeding.

Although feeding can often induce sleep, it can also interfere with it. The growth spurts babies experience between 1–3 and 6–8 weeks, and again at 3 months, compel them to feed more. They may not settle well until their hunger is fully satisfied and may wake sooner for yet more food to nourish their growing bodies! But as they grow bigger, their periods of sleep grow longer.

A baby's distinction between day and night that started at a couple of weeks is becoming well developed by 6–8 weeks of age. This is underpinned by a natural tendency to sleep for longer stretches of time.

By 3 months your baby will be increasingly stimulated by his surroundings and skilled at recognizing cues from his parents. He will therefore understand what is happening, making it the perfect time to introduce a bedtime routine, if you haven't done so already. As his sleep patterns are maturing, he will probably also fall into deep sleep within 10 minutes of settling.

His sleep cycle has now extended to 90 minutes, where it will remain for the rest of his life. This means he will rouse less often in sleep and this helps him to sleep for longer periods of 7–8 hours at night. He will probably be sleeping about twice as long at night as in the day.

Given all these fundamental and potentially disruptive changes, it is perhaps surprising that three-quarters of babies are sleeping through the night by 3 months of age.

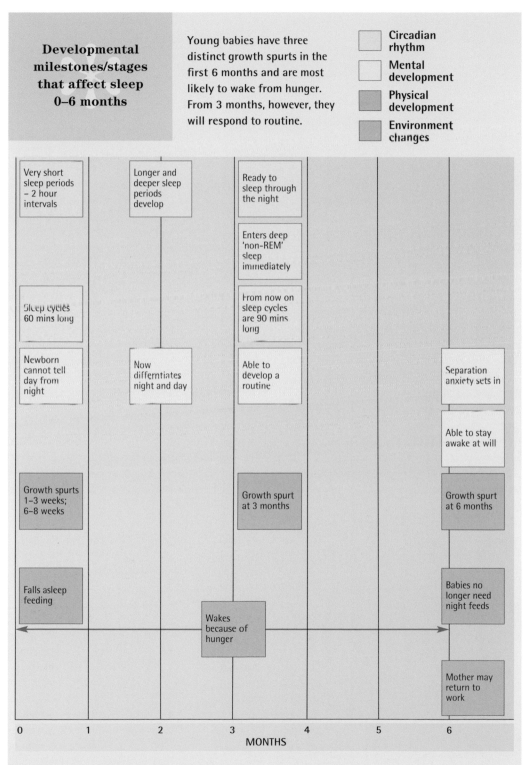

Developmental milestones/stages that affect sleep 0–6 months

Young babies have three distinct growth spurts in the first 6 months and are most likely to wake from hunger. From 3 months, however, they will respond to routine.

Circadian rhythm

Mental development

Physical development

Environment changes

Very short sleep periods – 2 hour intervals

Longer and deeper sleep periods develop

Ready to sleep through the night

Enters deep 'non-REM' sleep immediately

Sleep cycles 60 mins long

From now on sleep cycles are 90 mins long

Newborn cannot tell day from night

Now differntiates night and day

Able to develop a routine

Separation anxiety sets in

Able to stay awake at will

Growth spurts 1–3 weeks; 6–8 weeks

Growth spurt at 3 months

Growth spurt at 6 months

Falls asleep feeding

Babies no longer need night feeds

Wakes because of hunger

Mother may return to work

0   1   2   3   4   5   6

MONTHS

6–12 months

The age of 6 months marks a turning point as babies go on to solid food. This means that they no longer require night feeds and hunger is no longer a reason to wake. That is not to say they will not want a feed when they wake, but parents can reassure themselves that this is out of habit and not nutritional need. Some babies may have already dropped feeds at night but, for those who have not, the half-year mark is a cue to do so.

Although many babies will have settled into a bedtime routine by now, this can all too readily be disrupted by psychological and environmental changes.

The main psychological hurdle here is separation anxiety. It may seem strange that babies are not at their most anxious when they are most vulnerable, that is, when they are newborn. But their anxiety increases as their social awareness develops, often before their memory has caught up. They know when a person is leaving but cannot be sure from experience that they will always come back. The trauma can be repeated when the baby wakes in the night. Many babies are naturally anxious at this age, so try not to let it compound any guilt you may feel about returning to work around this time.

This anxiety can make bedtime difficult, as your baby gets upset when you leave her alone. The answer is not to stay with her until she falls asleep, which can create sleep problems (see page 52, Common sleep problems and their causes), but to return regularly to reassure and comfort her briefly until she eventually falls asleep alone.

There are many developments during this period and, as one cause of disturbance subsides, another often arises to take its place.

Somewhere around 6 months, teething starts. Although babies vary in the amount of pain they experience and the resulting complaints they make, almost all will protest at the discomfort. This often happens at night and needs to be dealt with in a matter-of-fact way in order not to create a dependency on a parent's prolonged presence at night (see page 47, Teething.)

Babies also become much more mobile between 6 and 9 months, first sitting and then crawling. If your baby moves in this way when she partially wakes at night, she may be disturbed and woken up completely by her movements.

By the end of this period, she will probably be able to stand up in her cot. If she is being left to get herself back to sleep, her protests can be quite upsetting as she strains on the bars of her cot like a distraught prisoner. But again, this will not last for many nights if you don't indulge it (see page 84, What if my baby stands up in the cot?).

The loss of the afternoon nap for most babies will mean that they are physically very ready to sleep when taken to bed.

At 1 year, most babies are down to one nap a day.

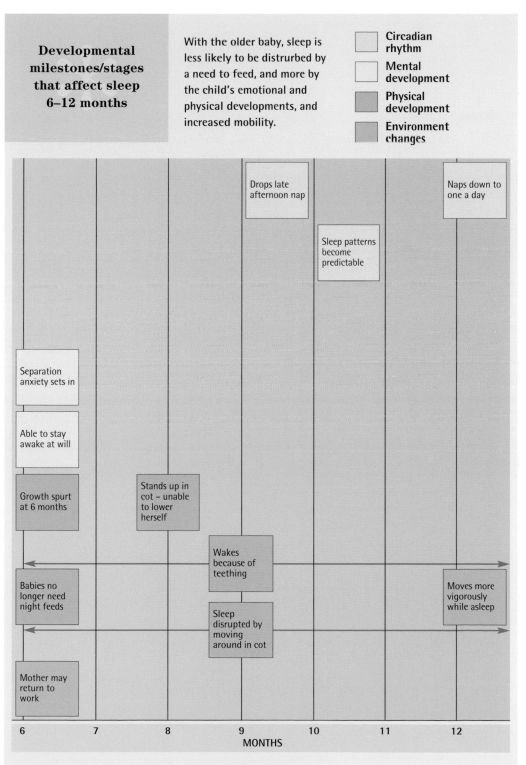

Developmental milestones/stages that affect sleep 6–12 months

With the older baby, sleep is less likely to be disturbed by a need to feed, and more by the child's emotional and physical developments, and increased mobility.

Circadian rhythm
Mental development
Physical development
Environment changes

Drops late afternoon nap

Naps down to one a day

Sleep patterns become predictable

Separation anxiety sets in

Able to stay awake at will

Growth spurt at 6 months

Stands up in cot – unable to lower herself

Wakes because of teething

Babies no longer need night feeds

Moves more vigorously while asleep

Sleep disrupted by moving around in cot

Mother may return to work

6   7   8   9   10   11   12
MONTHS

By the time your child attends school, she'll no longer need a daytime nap.

1–6 years

A baby's rapid maturation into a child makes this a fascinating period. The huge leaps in progress that occur are very rewarding for parents.

Naturally, there are benefits and disadvantages to this, although the disadvantages are usually temporary. A 1-year-old will begin to walk, for example, but this confers an independence that might not always be welcome at night. She may run away when you want to put her to bed, or even try to climb out of her cot.

Sleep disturbances, such as nightmares and sleep-talking, start to become apparent from about the age of 2 years. They peak at around 4 years but are something that most children grow out of (see page 54, Sleep disturbances).

The child's increasing independence can also be expressed in a stubborn insistence on keeping herself awake, even when you know she is very tired. This becomes more challenging to deal with in his second year, when she begins to talk and protest at your demands.

Around the age of 2½ years many children come out of nappies during the day. Most children are not dry at night until the age of 3½ years, but it is not uncommon for parents to delay removing the night nappies until much later if the child is not ready physically. Eventually, however, this has to be done,

and it is a rare child who never wets the bed (see page 62, Bed-wetting).

By the age of 3 years most children are beginning to forgo their daytime nap, and many are spending tiring hours at nursery, both of which should help promote a good night's sleep, if that is not already established.

The rapid development in a child's powers of imagination at this age often leads to fear of the dark, with accompanying images of monsters and witches exacerbating the anxiety. It is best to reassure your child that these fears are unfounded without resorting to looking for that monster under the bed or the goblin behind the curtains (see page 56, Nightmares and night terrors).

Going to nursery or school is a big step and can be one that aids good sleeping habits, as a child who has to get up at a given time in the morning is also a child who needs to go to bed at a reasonable time. There is evidence to show that many schoolchildren are getting insufficient sleep, while those who do get enough are more well behaved and perform better at school.

By the time they start school, all children have fully established circadian rhythms, so the dove-tailing of their social demands and biological ability to sleep well are well timed.

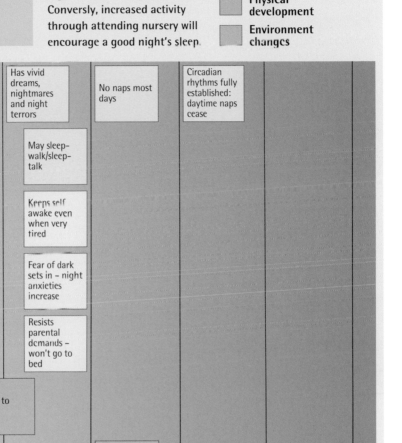

Developmental milestones/stages that affect sleep 1–6 years

A child's increasing ability to walk and talk can interfere with an established routine, as can nightmares and night terrors. Conversely, increased activity through attending nursery will encourage a good night's sleep.

- Circadian rhythm
- Mental development
- Physical development
- Environment changes

Naps down to one a day

Has vivid dreams, nightmares and night terrors

No naps most days

Circadian rhythms fully established: daytime naps cease

May sleep-walk/sleep-talk

Keeps self awake even when very tired

Fear of dark sets in – night anxieties increase

Resists parental demands – won't go to bed

Starts to speak

Coming out of night-time nappies – bed-wetting

Moves more vigorously while asleep

Moves from cot to bed

Goes to nursery

Goes to school

| 1 | 2 | 3 | 4 | 5 | 6 |

YEARS

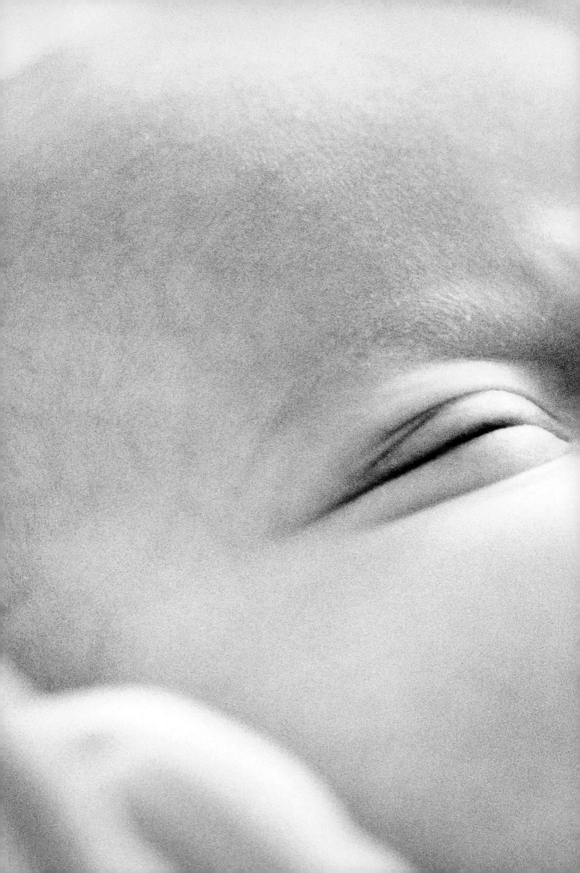

2

Encouraging good sleep habits

Preventing sleep problems

There are many successful ways to solve an existing sleep problem, as you will see, but it is even better to prevent the emergence of difficulties in the first place. By gradually and gently introducing a routine early in your baby's life, you can offset the effort of imposing one later, when he may well be more resistant.

Get into a rhythm: the first 3 months

A newborn is unable to tell night from day, cannot remember what happened to him an hour ago and will follow the mysterious internal rhythms with which he came into the world. He will alternately fall asleep, feed and lie back watching the world, as his needs dictate. But it is surprising just how soon he will respond to external cues, and it is this process in which you need to actively engage.

At a very rudimentary level you can start teaching your baby the difference between night and day from as young as 2 weeks (see opposite, Tell your baby the difference).

By 6 weeks you may notice that your baby is starting to become more settled. Less distracted by the novelty and strangeness of his environment, he will be communicating more openly with you. He will start to tell you more clearly when he needs to sleep (see Box, Sleep cues) and if you respond appropriately, you will be setting up a dialogue that will work over time to both your benefits.

The main advice in this crucial learning period is to settle your baby to sleep in his crib or cot while he is awake or drowsy, but not asleep. It is very tempting to rock, cuddle or feed a young baby to sleep. It works and it is quick: what more could a tired parent ask for! But it does not enable your baby to learn that he can get himself to sleep and this will make it more difficult to establish a routine early on.

So, follow the simple guidelines for young babies (see opposite, Tell your baby the difference) and try to settle him while he is awake or when he is drowsy but not yet asleep.

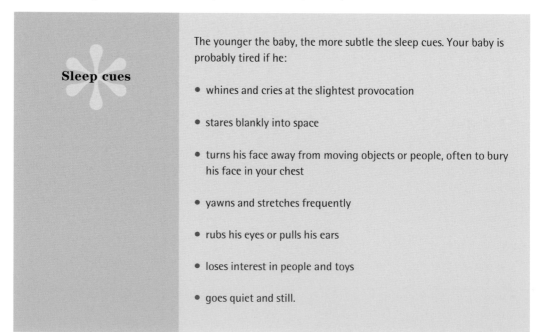

Sleep cues

The younger the baby, the more subtle the sleep cues. Your baby is probably tired if he:

- whines and cries at the slightest provocation

- stares blankly into space

- turns his face away from moving objects or people, often to bury his face in your chest

- yawns and stretches frequently

- rubs his eyes or pulls his ears

- loses interest in people and toys

- goes quiet and still.

By around 3 months, you should aim to have established a bedtime routine with your baby falling asleep without the aid of physical contact with you, your voice or even your presence. Babies who have learned to fall asleep independently by this age are also physically able to sleep through the night without waking for feeds.

Tell your baby the difference

You can help your baby to distinguish night from day, and sleep time from play time or rest time, in deliberate ways.

During the day

- Spend a lot of time interacting with him during his wakeful periods.

- Keep the curtains open and, when necessary, the lights on.

- Don't try to minimize noise around the house.

- Take him out for walks for plenty of fresh air and daylight.

- For naps, use a room that is not too dark and not too shielded from normal household sounds.

During the night

- Keep curtains drawn and noises down when you settle him for the night.

- Make sure his room is warm and cosy.

- Have a bedtime routine that includes changing him into night-time clothing.

- Keep night feeds as quiet, sleepy and as brief as possible; don't play or talk to him.

- If you have to go to him in the night, say the minimum required, keep the lights off or down, do not pick him up unless you think

Babies often rub their eyes when tired.

he is unwell and stay as short a time as necessary: be business-like.

- Only change his nappy if necessary.

Two teachers are better than one

The demands of a new baby, however well he sleeps for his age, can weaken the resolve of the firmest and most focused parent. If they are coupled with problems caused by a sleepless older sibling, you may well be too tired to follow through your sleep training for your baby. As a result, you risk ending up with two children with sleep problems.

By the time your baby arrives, you want your older child to be reasonably easy to settle at night and his sleep patterns to be predictable. You will then not only reduce your work at bedtime, but also have a child who will serve as the perfect role model for your new baby as he learns to sleep well.

Creating a sleep routine

A good sleep routine is the foundation on which the healthy sleep habits of a lifetime are built. Teaching your child to sleep well is the most basic lesson that she and you need to learn – and it is never too late.

Bedtime rules

A fixed bedtime routine has many advantages (see Table opposite).

However, the real benefits of a bedtime routine are enduring and, for most parents, well worth any short-term sacrifices they need to make. If you haven't followed a sleep routine with your baby and want to introduce it when she is older to help her sleep, you will need to be committed, focused and firm and it is never too late to do so.

As this will be part of your family life for some years, it is important that you and your partner are in agreement about it. As you are likely to share in its implementation, at least in part, it is also important that you agree on the detail as well as the general idea. What elements do you want to include, and in what order? (For some ideas for discussion, see Box, Routine recipe.)

Time for bed!

The timing of your bedtime routine is as important as its constituents. It should last no longer than 45 minutes; 30 minutes is often ample. If you start getting your child ready for bed too early, the whole procedure can lose focus. This often happens if the bedtime routine is not centred on the child's bedroom. If a child comes downstairs during this time, for example, it can break the bedtime spell.

This time should be spent pursuing predictable, low-key activities around the child's bedroom area. Anything that stimulates your child can disrupt the procedure, so avoid noisy games, sugary or caffeinated food or drinks, or exciting play with a parent returning from work.

Set your child's bedtime and plan to start the routine about half an hour beforehand, so that she picks up all the cues and is sleepy as you complete it. Once you have left her, she should take no more than 10–15 minutes to fall asleep.

Bedtime routine: advantages and disadvantages

Advantages	Disadvantages
It sets up the expectation of sleep so that the child is more willing to wind down at bedtime.	It can be tedious to implement because of its restrictive and repetitive nature.
It provides an atmosphere of familiarity and security that is conducive to calm rest before sleep.	It suppresses spontaneity.
It ensures the child goes to bed in time to get enough sleep for her age.	It can directly conflict with sudden work or social demands in the early evening.
It involves the child and encourages her to take responsibility for her behaviour.	It takes commitment and dedication.
It sets up positive sleep associations (see page 53).	

Routine rules

Plan your routine carefully.

- Base your starting time on what fits in with your family life: if you are realistic, you are more likely to keep to it.

- Consider what time you want your child to wake up, taking into account nursery or school starting times if they apply; work around a notional 11 hours sleep and time your routine accordingly.

A massage can soothe a restless baby before bedtime.

Routine recipe

Families favour different bedtime routines. The following are typical elements of bedtime routine, which you can combine and adapt to suit your child's needs:

- a bath

- massage and quiet music

- getting into nightclothes

- story-telling

- a cuddle and goodnight kiss.

- Talk to your partner about whether one or both of you want to be involved in the routine – which may depend on whether you work and for how long – because this may affect the starting time.

- The purpose of the bedtime routine is to prepare your child for sleep. Therefore it should be calm, relaxing and focused.

- Children need clear boundaries in most of their activities, and bedtime is certainly no exception.

- Even though it is important to know the bedtime rules, the bedtime routine is an opportunity for you and your child to enjoy spending time together. It is important to make it pleasurable, so that your child looks forward to going to bed.

Naps

Naps are vital to babies and young children, and it is a mistake to think that daytime sleep is less important than the sleep they get at night. In fact, at 3 months old, 30 per cent of a baby's sleep occurs in the daytime. Although this declines with age, the reduction is very gradual and, even at 9 months old, many babies are still relying on naps for 20 per cent of their sleep.

Daytime naps confer a number of concrete benefits on your child:

- He will sleep better at night.

- He will have a better appetite, particularly just after a nap.

- His moods will be more stable.

- A regular daytime sleep routine will make a bedtime routine easier.

- Dreaming sleep, or REM sleep (see page 18), which facilitates mental organization, often occurs during nap times.

- His concentration will improve.

- He will be generally happier and easier to manage.

Spacing: the key to good naps

Although a significant proportion of your child's sleep will occur in the day, it is just as important to focus on the time between these naps as it is on the length of the nap itself. If you space the naps well, the timing should take care of itself.

Naps need to be spaced so that the child naps properly when the time comes. A baby or toddler who catnaps frequently and does not spend long asleep on any occasion will not reap the same benefits from sleep as one who has fewer but longer naps. Your child may follow the same sleep/wake pattern at night, waking frequently.

This is partly to do with the length of the natural sleep cycle. While a night-time cycle is around 90 minutes (or 60 minutes in very young babies; see page 18, Sleep cycles), in the daytime this shrinks to about 45 minutes. It follows that a nap of, say, 30 minutes, will not provide the child with the full physiological benefits. Aim for one of your child's naps to be two cycles long, that is, 90 minutes. It is generally best to do this around midday, especially as this is the nap that your child will continue to have until he is about 3 years old.

However, while daytime naps generally benefit night sleep, they can be counterproductive if not spaced well or if taken too early or too late. Naps can be difficult to space when surrounding conditions encourage a baby or toddler to nod off at the 'wrong' time. This often happens in the car or pushchair and, if you have a schoolchild, may regularly occur on the school pick-up, for example.

A late afternoon nap can cause battles at bedtime, whereas a nap taken very early in the morning can contribute to early rising problems. You can alter these times gradually over a period of a few days by slowly moving the nap time forwards or backwards by 10–15 minutes every 2–3 days.

Also too much sleep in the day may mean your child will sleep less at night. Children will only sleep for a certain numbers of hours in every 24 hours and their day/night sleep requirements may be put out of balance if their naps are too long.

If you feel the need to change your child's napping schedule, it can help to introduce a routine. This need not be as rigid or as lengthy as the night-time routine, but could include, for example, a nappy change, a drink, a look at a book and a cuddle. By keeping it brief and being consistent, you will teach your child to settle well during the day. Aim for your child to have at least one daily nap in his cot, or bed, until he is well into his third year of age.

Spacing naps in young babies Some young babies want to snack and nap, but do not get enough food to last them until the next mealtime, nor enough sleep to give them the energy to enjoy a wakeful period. There are two approaches to this.

1 Try increasing the time between naps very gradually. For example, if you want your baby to have a nap every 3 hours but he cannot go longer than 2 hours without falling asleep, delay the nap by 10–15 minutes every 2–3 days until you reach the desired time. If your baby gets very over-tired, you may have to slow down the process until he is ready to move on again. Be consistent with your pre-nap routine and your method of settling your baby.

2 At feeding times encourage your baby to take a full feed. If he begins to fall asleep while feeding, try winding him or changing his nappy before finishing the feed. Feeding times should become more efficient as the length between naps increases.

Naps and night-time

There is a popular myth about naps that needs to be dispelled: namely that, by reducing the length or number of daytime naps, you will lengthen the night-time sleep or reduce the number of times your child wakes in the night. This idea is particularly appealing to parents who have suffered broken nights over a long period of time or whose child wakes up very early every morning.

It is not a strategy that will work, however. A baby or toddler who is sleep-deprived in the day is likely to become irritable and over-tired as night-time approaches. This will not only make your bedtime routine considerably more difficult, but it is also likely to affect the quality of your child's night-time sleep. The level of cortisol, one of the main stress hormones, declines during sleep; conversely, it creeps up if a child is deprived of sleep. If your child is over-tired he may be stressed and find it difficult to relax at bedtime, he may struggle to go to sleep and have increased wakings at night.

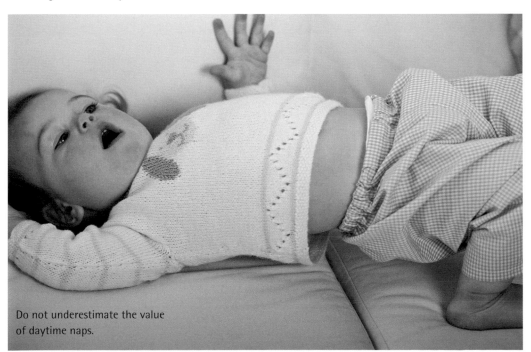

Do not underestimate the value of daytime naps.

Number and length of naps

This depends on the child's age. All children mature at different rates, but these are general guidelines.

- **0–3 months** A nap about every 2 hours. By 3 months, the total daily nap time should average 5 hours.

- **3–6 months** The time between naps will lengthen to 3 hours or more, meaning that your baby will have three or four regular naps a day. By 6 months, the total daily nap time should average 3–4 hours.

- **6–9 months** Three naps: two naps of about 45 minutes each in the morning and late afternoon and one of about 90 minutes around lunchtime. By 9 months, the total daily nap time should average 3 hours.

- **9–12 months** Down to two naps: the late afternoon nap can now be dropped, leaving one nap of about 45 minutes in the morning and another of 1½–2 hours after lunch.

Your baby should be awake by 3.30 pm. By 12 months, the average daily nap time should total 2½ hours.

- **12 months plus** Down to a single nap: the morning nap can now be dropped, leaving just one midday nap. Toddlers often find they are not tired enough for a morning nap and too tired to wait until after lunch, but you can easily solve this problem by temporarily bringing lunch forward (see opposite, Napping too much). At around this age, the average daily nap time should total 2 hours.

- **2–3 years** One daytime nap is usually sufficient throughout this period. Many children will have grown out of naps altogether by the age of 3 years. It is important to avoid a late afternoon nap, which can affect bedtime. Between 2 and 3 years, the average daily nap time totals 1 hour. When your child gets to 3 years, a 'power nap' may be sufficient.

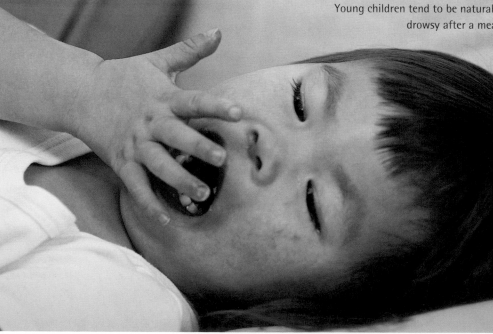

Young children tend to be naturally drowsy after a meal.

Napping problems

Many parents encounter problems with napping. The most common are outlined below, together with suggested solutions.

The short-napper Some babies settle well for naps but then wake after a brief sleep. This is because they have moved into the next sleep cycle (see page 18) into a brief wakening and are unable to go back to sleep. The key is to help your baby go straight back to sleep.

- Keep a diary of your baby's nap schedule, taking note of the length of the nap (see page 72, Keeping a sleep diary).

- If your young baby wakes regularly after 30 minutes, listen for signs of stirring or mumbles (a timer can be useful). Go into the room and stroke, pat or rock – what ever it takes – your baby back to sleep. In time, your baby should take longer naps without your help.

- If you are following a sleep programme and your baby wakes prematurely from a nap, use the same procedure that you use to settle him at bedtime.

- If you have an older baby, try not responding at all when he wakes – he may take himself back to sleep.

- Improvements can take a week or more. It is better to work on one nap at first. The lunchtime nap is ideal because it needs to be longer. If your baby is not asleep again within 45 minutes, abandon this nap to avoid upsetting the entire day's schedule.

Napping too much If your child is napping more than necessary for his age, this may have an affect his night-time sleep. The amount of sleep that he gets in 24 hours may not change but more of it will have shifted to the daytime.

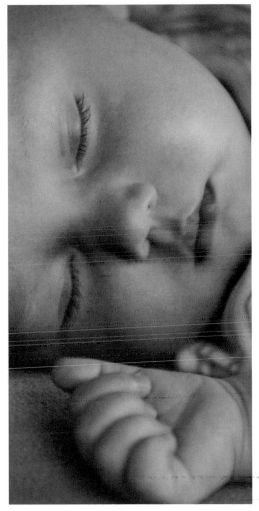

Young children often to fall asleep on car journeys, and this can affect their ability to nap.

Napping too early If his morning nap is too early, he may start waking early. Try shifting this nap by 10 minutes each day until your child is napping around 9.30–10 am.

As your child gets older and no longer needs a morning or late afternoon nap, delay and shorten it by 10 minutes each day until you can stop it completely.

The transition from two to one nap a day after 12 months is one that toddlers often find difficult. Try gradually cutting down the morning nap by 10 minutes each day and moving the afternoon nap to just after lunch to help your child adjust.

Creating the right environment

It is always best to accustom your child to sleeping naturally in your own domestic environment. Her bedroom needs to be conducive to sleep, but it should not be organized to meet special conditions without which she is unable to sleep. Simplicity is the key: you will then find it easier to recreate the conditions when you stay at the homes of family and friends or on holiday.

Noises off

Parents often worry about noises in or outside the house disturbing their child's sleep. However, children tend not to be as distracted by ambient noise as adults and, in general, once a baby or toddler is asleep it takes more than a thunderclap to wake them. Older children tend to be a little more sensitive. Nevertheless, it is still not a good idea to creep about, because relative silence is likely to make your child more sensitive to noises near her bedroom.

If you live on a busy road, the chances are that you have got used to the constant hum of traffic – and the same will probably apply to your baby or child. In fact, this is rather like the white noise produced by a vacuum cleaner or washing machine that young children often find strangely soothing.

Turn down the heat

Children do not need to be very warm to sleep. In fact, the ideal bedroom temperature is probably a little lower than it is in the rest of the house – about 18 °C (64 °F) is ideal.

Children often find it difficult to settle if they are very warm, and modern bedclothes, such as feather-filled duvets, tend to maximize heat retention around their bodies. These are not advised for babies under 1 year old, but if you use them for older children, you will not need to heat the bedroom much at night. Over-heating is a risk factor for cot death (see page 38, Sudden infant death syndrome). The best way to check the temperature of your baby's body is to feel her tummy or the back of her neck.

Comfort zone

Your child needs to feel secure and reassured in her bedroom in order to fall asleep there and stay asleep. You can help by placing familiar objects around her bed or cot. A happy family photograph on the wall at her bedside, for example, will provide a reassuring emotional backdrop to bedtime.

However, there can be a fine line between providing a comforting bedtime environment and creating inappropriate sleep associations. While a cuddle with your child as she settles may fall into the former category, the need for a cuddle every time the child wakes in the night is an inappropriate association that you will probably want to break (see page 53, Inappropriate sleep associations).

Lights out

Babies and children need to get used to sleeping in various light conditions, both in the dark, most probably when they rouse at night, and in the daylight, which may last until 10.00 pm in midsummer.

It is preferable to allow them to adjust to the natural seasonal light or dark, rather than trying to modify it all year round. However, if your child tends to resist bedtime and gets up early in the light summer months, thickly lined curtains can help.

Fear of the dark

A comfort blanket may help your child overcome fear of the dark.

There is perhaps no fear more common among children than that of the dark. It is particularly widespread among young, pre-schoolchildren, whose active imaginations can turn a bed into a cage or a shadow into a monster when the lights are out.

Although children eventually grow out of this fear naturally, in the meantime it can make them reluctant to go to bed and difficult to settle if they wake in the night. But there are steps you can take to help them overcome this fear more quickly.

- While reassuring your child that she is safe in her bedroom, talk to your child about what might make her feel more safe, such as a special toy or other comforter.

- Show your child that you understand but don't necessarily share her fears. For example, you can tell her: 'I know you feel scared but nothing will hurt you' or 'Don't worry, Mummy and Daddy are here'.

- Install a nightlight in your child's room, or leave a light on in the hallway so that some light filters into the room.

- Maintain a familiar and predictable bedtime routine to make her feel secure.

- Resist the temptation to check for monsters or intruders when your child goes to bed in an attempt to prove they are not there. This may only intensify her fantasy.

- In the morning, but never at night, ask her to describe her fears. Reassure her that you used to have very similar fears but soon grew out of them.

Safe sleeping

Before you think about how much your child is sleeping, whether he should be making it through the night, or doing with one nap or two, you may need to ask yourself a more basic question: is he safe? Your choice of furniture, bedding and sleeping arrangements primarily influence how well he sleeps each night, but they can also affect his health.

Sudden infant death syndrome (SIDS)

These are the words that many parents, especially new ones, fear most. In fact, despite its wide media coverage, SIDS – or cot death, as it is more commonly known – affects one in 2,000 babies. Therefore the risks to any individual family are small. However, you will want to do your best to avoid becoming a significant part of this statistic.

While there has been a lot of research into SIDS in the past 20 years, no clearly identifiable cause has been found. Fortunately, however, a lot is known about the risk factors and you can minimize your risk by observing the following six standard rules.

1 Back to sleep Lay your baby down on his back. A recent study showed that babies who were laid on their front had more breathing difficulties than those laid on their backs.

2 Feet to foot The bedding should be arranged so that your baby's feet are close to or touching the foot of the cot, to avoid them shuffling below the bedcovers and being smothered.

3 Not too hot Room heating is not required at night, except in severe winter weather. Babies' bedrooms should be kept a little cooler than the rest of the house, at around 18 °C (64 °F).

4 Smoke-free zone Smoking during pregnancy has been known for a long time to harm babies while they are in the womb. It is now accepted that smoking around a young baby can increase the risk of cot death, and the greater the exposure, the higher the risk.

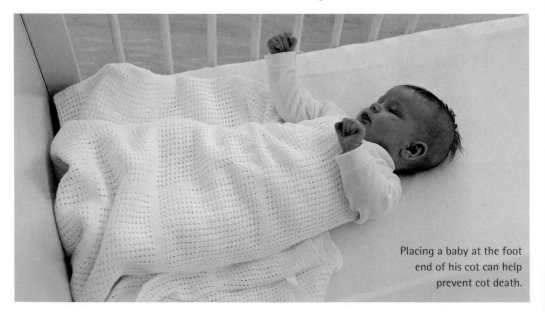

Placing a baby at the foot end of his cot can help prevent cot death.

Tips for co-sleepers

- Make sure there is no space between your mattress and the wall into which your baby could slip.

- Don't use duvets or eiderdowns on the bed if you have a young baby in it, and remove the pillow where he is sleeping.

- Only share your bed with your baby if you have enough room. If it is too cramped, your baby could get squashed or fall out.

- Never sleep with your baby if either you or your partner smokes, has recently drunk alcohol, taken recreational drugs, is on medication or excessively tired.

- If you are unsure about co-sleeping but want your baby physically near, you can use a bedside cot with the side removed as an extension of your bed space

- You can make a special 'baby space' in your bed, using your baby's own bedding.

5 Prompt medical advice Babies who become unwell, particularly if they have a raised temperature, breathing difficulties or are less responsive than usual, or any combination of these, should be seen immediately by a doctor.

6 Bedsharing for comfort, not sleep
Very young babies who sleep in their parents' bed are statistically at higher risk of cot death. However, this finding mainly applies to babies of parents who smoke, have been drinking or are on medication – or are excessively tired.

Co-sleeping

Co-sleeping is what nearly all parents used to do when most families were large and dwellings small. It still is the norm in many parts of the world, often for cultural rather than economic reasons. Whether or not to share your bed will be a matter of personal choice. Bear in mind that recent research concluded that parents should not bring a new baby into their bed for the first 8 weeks because, statistically, this is when he is at highest risk of cot death.

There are obvious attractions to sleeping in the same bed as your baby or toddler: it is comforting for both the parent and child, and the parent can deal with night waking or night feeding without the inconvenience of getting out of bed.

There are also disadvantages to co-sleeping. From the child's point of view, it can establish poor sleeping habits as the child becomes dependent on the parents' physical presence at night to sleep. It can also be over-stimulating for a baby or toddler, encouraging them to feed or search out your side of the bed when they would otherwise be asleep. In addition, you should never fall asleep with your baby on the sofa, as this increases the risk of sudden infant death (SIDS, see page 38).

From the parents' point of view, sharing a bed with an infant can cause poor sleep: a baby of around 4 months upwards tends to wriggle around a lot, disturbing others in the bed. He also has the potential to create problems in the parents' relationship, as they are able to have less physical contact.

If you do not want to co-sleep with your child, you can always allow your baby, toddler or child into your bed for a cuddle in the morning (after an agreed time!), and enjoy this physical time together.

Sleeping arrangements

Most young babies sleep in their parents' room, at least for the first few weeks of life. Parents feel that they can get to know their baby better this way and be there if she needs immediate attention. You may sleep more peacefully between feeds knowing she is all right and, of course, it saves you the disruption of leaving the room when the baby cries.

Where will your baby sleep?

There are no hard-and-fast rules about where you put your baby to sleep, as long as she is safe and comfortable, and circumstances will change as your child gets older. However, according to the guidelines for sudden infant death syndrome (SIDS; see page 38), it is best to have your baby in a cot in your own room for the first 6 months.

Once her sleeping patterns have settled, you may decide to move her into a separate room. This can be beneficial because your baby will become accustomed to falling asleep by herself. Make sure that the room is kept at a comfortable temperature (18 °C/64 °F), to avoid her over-heating and install a baby monitor if you are worried that you won't hear her crying during the night.

Some people take the view that an independent room is better, as sleeping in a separate room gives the parents space to be together, helps the baby learn to sleep on her own and means both parents and child are less likely to disturb each other.

From basket to bed

As your baby grows quickly in her first year or two, she is likely to progress through three or four items of sleeping equipment.

Moses baskets Many parents use these in the early days. They have the advantage of being both light and portable, so that you can transfer your baby into whichever part of the house you are currently occupying. To begin with, your baby may enjoy the

Keep it simple

Babies do not need the additional comforts that adults have in their beds and some can be positively dangerous for infants.

- **Do not use duvets, quilts or very thick blankets** These can cause over-heating. Depending on the temperature, it is advisable to use a cotton sheet and one to two thin cellular blankets. Only use duvets after your child's first birthday.

- **Never use hot-water bottles** Your baby does not need them and they are potentially dangerous; the same applies to electric blankets.

- **Use a firm mattress** Foam, hollow fibres, natural fibres or a sprung interior all provide sufficient firmness. The mattress should fit snugly to the base of the cot and have an easy-clean cover.

- **Do not use cot bumpers or a pillow** These can contribute to over-heating or even suffocate your baby.

Keep decoration in the nursery simple and with minimum night-time stimulation.

small, snug environment of a Moses basket. However, after just a few weeks, you may find that she can wake herself up as she becomes more active and her arms touch the sides as she sleeps. Make sure that the basket is stable – particularly if it is on a raised stand.

Cradles These are also an attractive option in the early days, because they are raised up and will be almost level with your bed. Many can be rocked, which young babies find very soothing. However, as always, you have to be careful not to encourage your baby to rely on being rocked to get to sleep, as this could set up inappropriate sleep associations. Most cribs can be locked into a stationary position, and you should probably do this to allow your baby to learn to fall asleep without being swayed from side to side.

Cots There are a great many varieties of cot. While some cots are a matter of taste, you need to ensure that the cot you are buying meets safety standards. There should be no horizontal bars, however, which

would enable the child to climb out when she is older. Almost all cots now have a drop-side mechanism, and you need to make sure that this is secure and cannot be opened by inquisitive little fingers.

Some cots also have an adjustable mattress level, starting high up for easy access in the first months, then finishing on the lowest level once your baby is able to sit up. The mattress should fit tightly in the cot frame; if you can slide two or three fingers between the cot sides or ends and the mattress, the mattress is too small.

Cot-beds These serve a dual purpose: you can use one as a large cot in the early years and then, by removing the sides, transform it into a small bed when your child is old enough. In this way, your child is less likely to have problems in moving to a 'big bed'.

You can tell if your child is ready for a 'big bed' when she seems cramped or tries to escape. As a guideline, once she is around 1 m (3 ft) tall, she should be in a bed (see also page 45, From cot to bed).

Adapting to circumstances

The basic rules for teaching a child to sleep better apply to all families, whatever their circumstances. While some sleep programmes may seem easier to apply under certain conditions, there is always a way to adapt to your particular circumstances. So don't be deterred by the apparent restrictions of your current situation. The principles throughout this book can be made to work for every family.

Living conditions
The size, arrangement and location of the place in which you live should not be viewed as a restrictive factor for how easy or difficult it is to apply certain techniques.

Sharing a room If your baby shares a room with you, some programmes, such as controlled crying, will be more difficult to apply: you can hear every sound the baby makes, and he can see you. A simple screen, such as a curtain, between your bed and his can at least create the impression of physical separation.

Environmental noise Constant noise, such as road traffic, is generally less distracting for a young child than it is for an adult, so don't regard this as a reason to postpone or abandon your sleep programme. If noise is disturbing your child, it is more likely to be sudden sounds, such as nearby doors being slammed. If you feel the need to reduce the impact of such ambient noise before starting a sleep programme, you could try using equipment that emits white noise – rather like the hiss of wind or splash of waves – thereby camouflaging other sounds.

No parent likes the sound of a baby crying for an hour or more. So if you share walls with your neighbours and are going to embark on a controlled crying programme, it helps to involve them by explaining what you are doing – and, of course, reassuring them that it should not last more than a few nights.

Siblings
Not all children with sleep problems are singletons. Some have siblings, and this can cause its own complications, although they are seldom inseparable. At Millpond Children's Sleep Clinic, we deal with all age groups and all sizes of family.

Temporary separation may be the answer to siblings who disturb each other at night.

Second- and third-time parents may be in the habit of rushing in to a baby or toddler if he cries or calls out in the night, not out of anxiety, like a new parent, but to ensure that the older child is not woken up by the noise.

The fear of disturbing an older child can also make you postpone the treatment of a younger one. If you have a baby with a sleep problem and a school-age child, for example, you may be reluctant to impose a controlled crying programme for fear of interrupting the older child's sleep, especially if they have adjacent rooms. In this case, you have a number of choices: you can simply wait until a school holiday, if it is not far off; you can temporarily move the older child further away from the baby at night; or you can move the baby's cot to another part of the house. Alternatively, you can choose a method, such as gradual retreat (see page 76), that usually involves less crying (see also page 136, Solution 12).

You don't want to create rivalries or antagonisms that could result in the older child behaving badly, especially at night if she is currently a good sleeper. It can be a good idea to involve the older child in your plans: she will then feel part of what you are doing and be more prepared to cooperate.

Work

If you work, you will be used to forward planning and that is just what you need to do if you are to solve a sleep problem while continuing to work.

If you have yet to return to work, you should ideally start solving the sleep problem 2 months or more before you go back. This will allow time for the baby to learn a new way of sleeping and both of you to settle into and reinforce the new sleep pattern.

If you are already at work when your child develops a sleep problem, then nip it in the bud if possible. With competing demands on your energy, this can be a difficult step, but one for which you will be rewarded. Sleep problems are invariably quicker to cure the earlier you start.

Once you have decided on the approach you are going to take, aim to start applying it at the end of the following working week. You can expect to have a couple of very disrupted nights at first, but you then at least have the next day to recover without the additional demands of work.

Similarly, wait until you have a clear few days at work without major demands before starting a sleep programme. All techniques will deprive you of some sleep to start with.

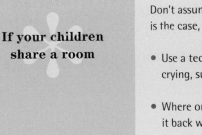

If your children share a room

Don't assume that one child will disturb the other. If you think this is the case, consider the following options:

- Use a technique with gradual, small changes that involve less crying, such as gradual retreat.

- Where one child is in a cot, move this out of the room and bring it back when the child with the problem is sleeping better.

- If the older child is a sound sleeper, move her out of the bedroom, perhaps to 'camp out' in another room if another bed is not available. You can make this fun, with a sleeping bag and favourite toys around. Be sure to explain that this is only for a night or two.

- Get the cooperation of the older child by giving her a sense of responsibility and engaging her in the 'game' of seeing how quickly you can both get the baby to sleep.

- If you have twins, try to treat the problem as one. As they have always been together, you may be surprised how readily they accommodate each other's sleep problems.

Times of change

Parents often feel that the worst is over once their child is sleeping routinely through the night. This is true to some extent, but circumstances change and any of a number of factors can disrupt this routine. These include the arrival of a new baby, holidays, moving house, moving from cot to bed and illness.

A new baby in the family

While many toddlers and children get excited about the arrival of a new baby, few are prepared for the emotional conflicts that it can cause. Older siblings often feel displaced, excluded and upstaged.

The anxieties that are generated often manifest themselves at night, resulting in bedtime battles and more frequent night waking. Whereas in the daytime these anxieties might come out in tantrums, at night-time the signs are more subtle. The older child may be more difficult to settle and call out for you more, creating excuses to win your attention.

The bottom line is to carry on as before as far as you can. Maintain your older child's routine as much as possible, continuing to spend special time with her, such as story-telling at bedtime. But don't get drawn into giving her special attention in the night. Making her feel valued is important but take the opportunities in the day to transmit these emotional messages so that you will not feel compelled to provide your presence at night.

This adaptation can start while you are in hospital. If your older child is coming to visit you, try to shift the spotlight away from the baby: get someone else to

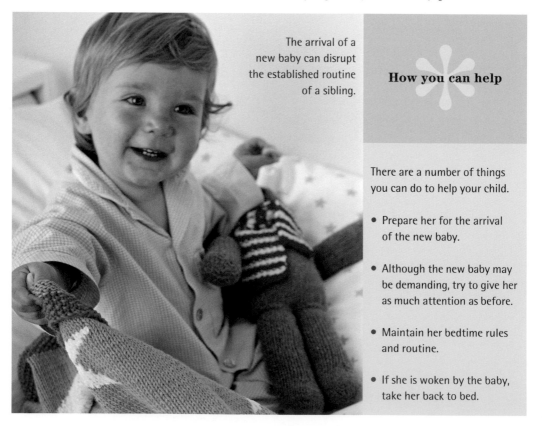

The arrival of a new baby can disrupt the established routine of a sibling.

How you can help

There are a number of things you can do to help your child.

- Prepare her for the arrival of the new baby.

- Although the new baby may be demanding, try to give her as much attention as before.

- Maintain her bedtime rules and routine.

- If she is woken by the baby, take her back to bed.

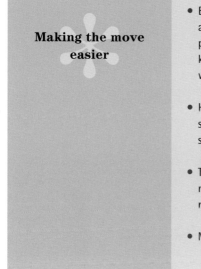

Making the move easier

- Even if you will be using the cot for your new baby, take it down a few weeks before he is due and replace it with a bed in the same position, so that the older child is certain of what is happening, knows there is no going back and has time to adapt and identify with her own space.

- Help to give your child a sense of occasion by, for example, putting special pictures on the wall by her bed or getting her to choose some new bed linen with you.

- Talk to her about her new bed; mention friends of hers who have made the shift to a big bed; show her pictures of big children in nice beds and small babies in cots.

- Maintain her usual bedtime routine.

hold him so that you can cuddle your child; give her a present to celebrate her new status as big sister. Once you are home, you can continue this by making her a special helper for the baby.

Eventually, as long as you stick to your night-time rules, any attention-seeking behaviour should pass.

From cot to bed

By the age of 3 years, most children are ready to move from their cot into a bed. There is no set age of course, and you need to watch out for the cues. More mobile toddlers, for example, may have already shown their readiness by climbing out of their cot. Other children, particularly those with older siblings, will have anticipated the change and begun to talk about having their own 'big bed'.

If your child is being moved out of her cot because you are expecting another baby, you can prepare her for the change. Don't leave it until the last minute. In the weeks before the baby is due, talk to her about the change and then involve her in decisions about the new bed. Where will it be? What bedclothes will she have? Where will you sit for her bedtime story? Discussing this will help her in the process of acclimatization.

If you do not move the older child into a bed before the birth, leave it until she has got used to having a new sibling.

The transition to a big bed is more difficult for some children than others. First children, for example, can be more attached to their cot, while subsequent children tend to be keen to emulate a big brother or sister and make the move more easily.

Sleep safety

When a child first moves into a big bed, it is not unusual for them to fall out. There are a number of precautions you can take to minimize any risk:

- Put a guard on the bed: guards can run the whole length of the bed or just part way down, which makes getting in and out of bed easier.

- If you do not have a bed guard put some padding on the floor – an old duvet or a folded rug will do – to ensure a soft landing.

- 'Childproof' the room with safety catches for cupboards and windows. Secure heavy furniture to the wall.

- Clear away large objects and toys from the floor.

- Consider putting a stair gate across the bedroom door to stop night-time wandering.

Holidays

Holidays, by their very nature, represent a break in normal routine, and children may find this difficult to deal with. For example:

- The child may have to share a room with his parents.

- Parents are more likely to respond to crying because they are worried about disturbing other people.

- Nap times and bedtimes are disrupted.

- Parents recognize that the child finds it difficult to sleep in unfamiliar surroundings and therefore are less likely to enforce rules.

- Changing time zones affect the child's body clock.

- On returning home, the child finds it difficult to readjust to the normal rules and routines.

How you can help There are a number of measures you can take to help the situation.

- If you are flying, try to travel during the day, preferably during nap times.

- Ask for adjoining rooms rather than sharing a room, preferably with a baby monitor.

- Take your child's favourite blanket or soft toy.

- As far as possible, keep to your normal nap time and bedtime routines, allowing a night or two for your child to adjust to any changes.

- Once you are home again, resume the normal routines straight away.

- If you have travelled across a time zone, try to adapt to the local time as soon as possible. This may involve juggling your child's nap times. By the same token, as soon as you get

A holiday should not be a break from your child's normal bedtime routine.

back from any holiday, return to your familiar home routine immediately. Unless you have been away for many weeks, it should only take 2–3 nights – even if they are difficult ones – for your baby or child to readjust.

Moving house

The approach when you move house is broadly similar to that which you would adopt for a holiday. It is all about minimizing disruption and maximizing familiarity by sticking to your usual routine.

If your child seems disoriented and disturbed by the move, it may be best to maintain the sleeping arrangements you had before, at least for a short period. If you have children who shared a room in their last house, let them do so for a time in their new house, even if you plan to give them their own rooms soon. If your toddler seems unsettled and had a cot in your room, you can keep it there, at least for a short period of time.

As always, the watchword is routine: stick to this as far as you can, whatever the sleeping arrangements.

Clock changes

Your child's sleep pattern may be distrupted for a few days. But you should aim to put your child to bed at the 'new' time straight away. If you feel you want to make gradual changes, move your child's bedtime earlier or later by 15 minutes a day to accomodate the time change.

Illness

When a child is ill, his nights can be disturbed by frequent waking. Even children who can sleep through a jet plane taking off may be kept awake by the discomfort of a fever, coughing or a stuffy nose.

If your child needs medication or frequent close attention from you during this episode, you may want to sleep near him. However, you should sleep in his room, rather than the other way around. If you bring him into your bed, you may set up expectations and unhelpful sleep associations that will prove difficult to break once he is well again.

You cannot expect to start a sleep programme when your child is ill, but keep up the bedtime routine; this will prove invaluable when he recovers and needs to start getting used to 'normal life' again.

If your sick child calls for you in the night, you cannot ignore him as you might do otherwise. Once you have established that he does not need medical attention, reassure him that you are there if he feels bad again, but be business-like. Do not pick him up unless he is evidently distressed.

If your child shows signs of sleep problems when he is unwell, and these continue to cause disruption after the illness has subsided, you need to act decisively and reinforce the old routine as quickly as possible. A few nights of perseverance should get you back on track.

For more detailed information on specific illnesses that commonly affect sleep, see page 58, Other problems affecting sleep.

Teething

Your baby's first teeth will appear at some time between the age of 5 and 9 months. It can be difficult to know whether the unsettled behaviour you are seeing is due to teething, a minor illness or a new developmental stage. Teething runs a different course in individual babies and toddlers. Some fortunate children sprout teeth with barely a murmur but most, to varying degrees, find it an uncomfortable and often distressing experience.

Clearly, your child will grow out of it, but in the meantime you can help to alleviate the pain. Remedies include gum gel, homeopathic teething granules, cold food (such as cucumber) on which he can bite, and a teething ring. In extreme circumstances you can use children's pain-killers, but this is best avoided as the teething will continue sporadically for some time.

In other respects, you should treat the night-time waking or settling problems as you would for an illness (see above).

Knowing when your child is ill and what to do

It can be difficult to tell whether a very young baby is ill, but apparent illness at this age must be taken seriously, as symptoms can develop very quickly. Always call the doctor if your child:

- is under 3 months and has a temperature over 38 °C (100 °F)

- has a fever you cannot control

- has trouble breathing

- is under 12 months old and is vomiting and/or has diarrhoea

- is listless and off his food.

20 sleep habits – dos and don'ts

The reasons some children don't sleep well are often very simple and practical. If you are unsure why your child has difficulty getting to sleep or staying asleep, go through this checklist. You may find that you have overlooked one of the basic rules and that implementing it could make all the difference. If there is one page you should earmark in the book, it is probably this one.

Do ...

1 **Do establish a regular bedtime** This will regulate your child's body clock and ensure healthy sleep/wake patterns.

2 **Do avoid stimulating activities in the hour before bedtime** You can start building a brief routine into your child's pre-bedtime period from as early as 3 months, but always keep it low-key and relaxing.

3 **Do stick to a set bedtime routine** A bedtime routine might include: quiet play; a bath; a story; then lights out and a purposeful 'goodnight'. Make it low-key and relaxing. It should take no longer than 45 minutes.

4 **Do enforce clear boundaries for bedtime behaviour** This applies to you as well as your child! If you have said you will give him a cup of milk in bed, don't be talked into fetching a second. Once boundaries start to get stretched, most children will push at them more.

5 **Do place your baby in his cot when he is drowsy, not asleep** Try this as soon as you see the opportunity. If your baby can get used to falling asleep without your presence, he is likely to wake and demand you far less frequently.

A baby is usually asleep within 15 minutes of being put in his cot.

6 Do leave your child awake when you say goodnight This will encourage him to learn to get himself to sleep, which will benefit both of you.

7 Do aim for your child to be asleep within 15 minutes of leaving him This is the maximum amount of time it should take your child to fall asleep. If he is still awake, he may be having a nap too late in the afternoon or his bedtime routine may be too stimulating or insufficiently focused.

8 Do try to keep daytime naps regular and consistent This not only helps to establish predictable times, which can benefit you, but is also likely to make him a better sleeper at night.

9 Do keep the bedroom at a comfortable temperature The room doesn't need to be any warmer than 18 °C (64 °F), which is probably a little lower than the rest of the house. Children sleep better at a temperature slightly below rather than above average.

10 Do keep ambient noise down This means avoiding sudden, sharp sounds rather than tip-toeing about. It only really matters for the first 15 minutes after lights out: by then your child should be in a deep sleep.

Don't ...

11 Don't allow your child to take a nap after 3.30 pm from around 9 months of age A late afternoon nap can steal sleep from the night-time and make him more difficult to settle.

12 Don't give your child any stimulating food or drinks in the evening This includes drinks, such as tea, coffee and cola, as well as sweet foods. Both caffeine and sugar are stimulating.

13 Don't put your child to bed hungry Most children will settle better, and be less likely to rise very early, if they have eaten well in the day.

14 Don't create a settling routine that relies on props or requires your presence When your baby wakes at night, he may need them to be able to get back to sleep. Particular objects, such as a dummy, or interactions, such as a cuddle can become sleep associations (see page 53, Inappropriate sleep associations).

15 Don't bring your child into the living area during or after his routine This breaks the focus of your bedtime routine and sends mixed messages to your child, which he will find confusing.

16 Don't feed or soothe your young baby to sleep every night This is easily done, especially with very young babies, and rarely fails. But it can create a rod for your own back if he is later unable to settle without a feed.

17 Don't respond to repeated calls for attention after saying goodnight Most requests for a drink, a kiss or another trip to the toilet are excuses to string out bedtime and should be resisted so that they don't become a habit.

18 Don't rush to your baby or toddler when he cries or calls for you in the night As long as you know he is well, you should wait to see whether he settles himself. Constantly providing him with your presence could create or sustain sleep problems.

19 Don't use bedtime to discuss any difficulties relating to today or tomorrow This may unearth difficulties or anxieties from your child's day, which can interfere with sleep and are best discussed in the daytime. Try to get it out of the way at teatime.

20 Don't send your child to his bedroom as a punishment If your child is to become a good and independent sleeper, he needs to feel that his bedroom is a place of harmony and rest.

3

Understanding sleep problems

Common sleep problems and their causes

Although each child with a sleep problem exhibits it in his own way, the underlying causes fall into a small number of general categories.

The origins of sleep disruptions can originate from a variety of factors, from a child who has never learned to go to sleep by himself to a child who has been recently disturbed by an illness, holiday or a new baby. In their efforts to get their child to sleep parents may be inadvertently perpetuating their child's night-time behaviour by their actions.

The child's own stage of development – and the difficulties he experiences on the way – will influence when and how sleep problems first emerge. The three factors that can sustain or limit them are what happens during the day, how bedtime is handled, and what happens when a child wakes at night.

It is not a good idea to make a habit of settling with your baby.

Summary

Daytime napping Babies and young children need to nap during the day. However, if those naps are at the wrong time or of the wrong length, sleep problems can occur at bedtime, later on in the night and during the day (see page 32, Naps).

Bedtime battles Settling a child for sleep determines the course of the night to come. Problems with settling routines and behaviour are a common source of night-time disruption (see page 30, Creating a sleep routine).

Night waking All children wake in the night, however briefly. Waking is not the problem. It is the child's ability to get back to sleep unaided that makes the difference between a calm night and a disturbed night for both you and your child.

Night feeding Obviously young babies need to feed at night. However, some develop night-feeding habits that are not biologically necessary and that cause major disruption for the baby and the parents.

Sleep-phase problems Another category of sleep problem is when the timing of night-time sleep shifts forwards or backwards from what is normal – or at least convenient – so that the child is sleeping and waking too early or late.

Nightmares and night terrors Finally, there are sleep disturbances that involve actual or apparent extreme anxiety for the child. These are sporadic and unpredictable episodes, to be managed as and when they occur.

Inappropriate sleep associations

Getting a baby or child to sleep is not necessarily instinctive – for the parent or the child. When it proves difficult to achieve, parents often resort to on-the-spot aids to facilitate the process. These can be: physical interactions with the child, such as rocking, stroking or lying down on the child's bed; material objects, such as a special blanket or a dummy; less tangible things, such as singing and whispering.

A child who cannot fall asleep without these conditions being present, and who needs a parent to help recreate them when he rouses in the night, has inappropriate sleep associations.

They are not uncommon: about a fifth of babies and toddlers are unable to get back to sleep when they rouse in the night. This happens more often than you might imagine, as most children wake, or come close to waking, four or five times in the night.

Inappropriate sleep associations can be learned from birth, typically when parents rock or feed a baby to sleep on each occasion. The associations then continue because the parents reinforce the baby's dependency on this interaction by repeating it every time they want the baby to sleep. However, inappropriate sleep associations can start after some upheaval or disturbance. This often happens after a holiday, when the child has slept with the parents, or after an illness, when the child has been given attention each time he has woken.

Once learned, these associations persist even after the original difficulties that caused them have disappeared. If they are not addressed, they can then cause other sleep problems, such as bedtime battles.

Stopping the association

A child with inappropriate sleep associations needs to learn to fall asleep by himself at bedtime without any props. He should also be able to resettle himself in the night whenever he wakes.

Maintaining a sound, regular bedtime routine – or introducing one if you have not done so already – can help your child to learn a new set of appropriate sleep associations. You may find some of the techniques in Chapter 4 useful (see also page 48, Dos and don'ts).

As with other sleep solutions, expect a few difficult nights at the beginning. However, it is worth persisting: you, as well as your child, will get much better sleep and you will both gain an independence.

Does your child have inappropriate sleep associations?

It can be difficult to know whether your child is waking for this reason or because something else is disturbing him. The signs of inappropriate sleep associations are:

- inability to settle unless specific, familiar conditions are met

- frequent night waking

- crying or calling out for you whenever he wakes

- inability to settle himself when he rouses at night

- the ability to return to sleep quickly once a prop is put back in place.

Sleep disturbances

Alarming though they can be for parents, sleep disturbances are a normal developmental stage through which the vast majority of children pass unharmed.

Like adults, children go through various stages of sleep each night (see page 18, Sleep cycles). The transition between these stages can cause a child to partially wake. It is at these times that they are susceptible to various forms of sleep disturbance. The most widely recognized of these partial arousals are sleep-talking and sleep-walking.

They are most common after the age of 2 years and affect boys more than girls, with around 70 per cent of children experiencing sleep disturbances at some time.

There is little you can do about most of these disturbances, which are usually just manifestations of a maturing neurological system. However, some are exacerbated by sleep deprivation, so ensuring your child gets all the sleep she needs will help in this respect, as in so many other sleep problems.

Sleep-talking

A lot of people mumble occasional words while they are sleeping but this very rarely indicates a sleep problem. Children are more likely to talk while asleep because the linguistic centres of their brains are so highly stimulated, particularly in their early pre-school years. Most children will grow out of this common sleep disorder.

Sleep-walking

This is one of the forms of sleep disturbance that most concerns parents, because of the perceived risk of the child injuring herself while moving around in the night. In fact, the risk of this is relatively low, but if your child is a sleep-walker you can decrease this risk further by taking safety precautions (see Box, Precautions for sleep walkers).

Sleep-walking usually occurs about an hour after bedtime, when the child has entered slow-wave, non-REM sleep (see page 18). There is no set pattern: it can last for 5 minutes or 20, and the child can appear very calm or quite agitated.

Whatever the case, it is best not to intervene, as waking a child in this condition is likely to disorient and upset her. It is best simply to guide your child gently back to bed and stay in the room while she settles. Most children will have grown out of sleep-walking by the age of 6 years.

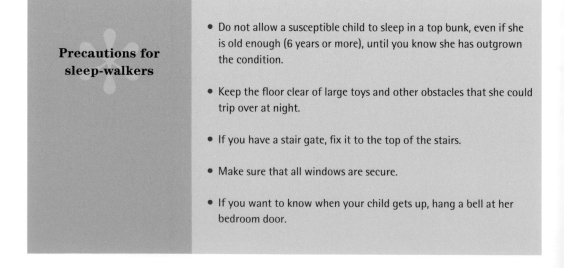

Precautions for sleep-walkers

- Do not allow a susceptible child to sleep in a top bunk, even if she is old enough (6 years or more), until you know she has outgrown the condition.

- Keep the floor clear of large toys and other obstacles that she could trip over at night.

- If you have a stair gate, fix it to the top of the stairs.

- Make sure that all windows are secure.

- If you want to know when your child gets up, hang a bell at her bedroom door.

Rhythmic movement disorder

As any parent who has had a toddler in bed with them will have learned to their cost, young children do not stay still when asleep. Tossing, turning, and sometimes total inversion – creating a footrest of your pillow – are all to be expected.

In rhythmic movement disorder, this tendency is taken a stage further. Symptomatic movements include recurrent head-banging, head-rolling, body-rocking and shuffling on hands and knees. Unless the head-banging has been so vigorous as to produce bruises, the child will not be aware of this having happened, even if the movements wake her up in the night. Most children will have outgrown these behaviours by the time they are about 4 years old.

Meanwhile, there are measures you can take to prevent or limit this behaviour.

- Do not respond at night with excessive concern; in fact, ignore it if possible.

- Ensure that your child has plenty of rhythmical activities in the day, for example, on playground equipment.

- Give your child plenty of attention in the day, so that you feel more able to ignore the night-time behaviour.

- If you feel emotional anxieties may play a part, talk to your child about these and offer reassurance. You may need to discuss this with your doctor.

Snoring

Snoring can be a sign of obstructive sleep apnoea – a condition more familiar to mothers than fathers, because it affects men more than women. In this case, it is a symptom of a physical blockage to the airways, which interrupts the normal breathing pattern. In adults, it is commonly caused by excess fat around the neck, which compresses the airways. It is also becoming more common in children as a result of an increase in childhood obesity.

However, snoring in young people is more likely to be caused by other conditions, including enlarged

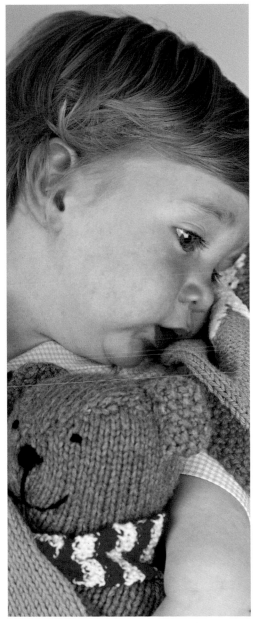

Sleep disturbances are common and rarely continue beyond 6 years of age.

tonsils, upper airway infection, hay fever, a blocked nose or a narrow pharynx (the airway running down from the nose). The repeated interruption to sleep that it causes results in daytime sleepiness.

A child who snores habitually, whether or not she has any of these conditions, should see a doctor.

Nightmares and night terrors

Both these forms of sleep disturbance sound equally distressing but, in fact, they are quite distinct (see Table opposite) – and the child will only be aware of one of them.

Although most nightmares and terrors in children are usually nothing to worry about, if several major episodes occur over a period of time, it is advisable to seek help as they could be caused by stress, which may require a doctor's attention.

Nightmares Nightmares occur in REM or 'dreaming' sleep (see page 18). As a result, they usually happen in the second half of the night, when REM sleep becomes more frequent. Nightmares are very common in young children, reaching a peak between the ages of 3 and 6 years, when about a quarter of children have at least one nightmare a week. However, they can happen in children as young as 2 years.

As most of us will remember, common themes are being chased by a large person or animal, or being stuck somewhere and unable to escape. While the themes are extreme and frightening, nightmares are perfectly normal reactions to the stresses and strains of growing up. Although they are caused by a healthy development of the imagination, it is unwise to stimulate this further by entering into the fantasy.

Your child is quite likely to call out or come to you in some distress when he has had a nightmare. The best thing to do is to listen to and reassure him and, if necessary, to stay with him until he has calmed down. It is important to remember that children under the age of 4 to 5 years cannot tell the difference between a dream and reality, so it is more important to comfort them than to try to offer a rational explanation.

If a child has recurrent nightmares about the same thing, it can be useful to talk through this the next day and help your child to think up a happy ending. Reassure him that it is a nightmare and will go away – and that you are there for him.

Night terrors Night terrors affect mainly pre-school children and occur in deep sleep. Of all the forms of sleep disorders, it is these that most disturb

Causes and prevention of night terrors

- **Sleep deprivation** A child who is sleep-deprived is more likely to have night terrors as he has a greater need for deep sleep. It is in the transition between this and the next stage of moderately deep sleep that night terrors may occur. Regular daytime naps and a constant bedtime (see page 30, Creating a sleep routine) will help to stabilize the biological clock.

- **Stimulants** Food or drink containing caffeine or a lot of sugar can over-stimulate the child and exacerbate any predisposition he may have to terrors, so should be avoided close to bedtime.

- **Stress** Although it is seldom the cause in young children, a significant stress in the family can contribute to the occurrence of night terrors. If you suspect this may be the case, try to address the issue separately.

- **Sleep cycle development** Young children have a very deep non-REM sleep stage, which alters as their sleep cycles mature (see page 18, Sleep cycles). Therefore, most children will naturally outgrow night terrors around the age of 5 or 6 years.

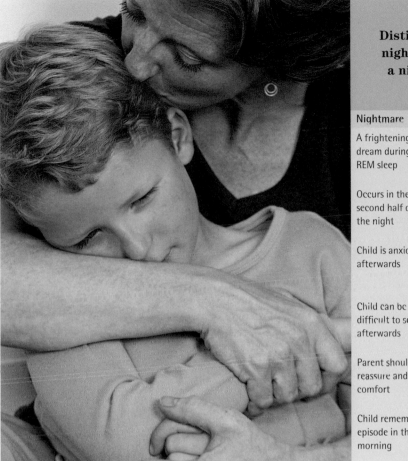

Distinguishing a nightmare from a night terror

Nightmare	Night terror
A frightening dream during REM sleep	A partial waking from non-REM sleep
Occurs in the second half of the night	Occurs early in the night
Child is anxious afterwards	Child is calm afterwards
Child can be difficult to settle afterwards	Child returns to sleep quickly afterwards
Parent should reassure and comfort	Parent should do little or nothing
Child remembers episode in the morning	Child remembers little or nothing

Alway comfort and reassure a child suffering from a nightmare.

parents, and understandably so. A young child experiencing a night terror is liable to 'wake up' suddenly out of a deep sleep, often with a wide-eyed, frightened expression, and sometimes he will scream loudly. In extreme cases, he may run around in a state of inconsolable anxiety.

Ironically, while these terrors may leave parents anxious, they do not disturb children. Although they may show all the signs of being terrified, this does not seem to register with them emotionally. Also, as they occur in deep sleep, the child is very unlikely to remember them after he wakes up.

Night terrors usually occur in the early part of sleep, sometimes as soon as half an hour after its onset. Any disturbance that causes the child to get out of bed in the first 2 hours of sleep is likely to be a night terror. Other tell-tale symptoms are thrashing around, sweating, crying or moaning.

A night terror rarely lasts more than a matter of minutes and the best response is simply to wait until it passes and, if the child does not get back into bed himself, guide him back to it. Do not attempt to wake the child, who will not benefit from comfort or reassurance and is more likely to be upset if roused from this state.

If the child has regular night terrors, rousing him from his deep sleep in the early part of the night – perhaps as you go to bed – may prevent a terror occurring. You can probably find out from your sleep diary (see page 72) when this occurs. You do not need to wake him, just stir him to interrupt the deep sleep cycle (see page 152, Solution 20).

Other problems affecting sleep

Some conditions that affect many children in their early lives can interfere with sleep. Although they are not sleep problems as such, they cause discomfort at night, which can wake the child or make it difficult for her to settle. You may be advised to give your child extra attention at night but, by doing so, you may risk creating inappropriate sleep associations (see page 53) and rewards for waking. So, ideally, you need to deal with these problems so that you can manage your child's sleep with minimal disruption.

Colic and reflux

Both these conditions are very common and are related to the baby's immature digestive system.

Colic is a condition characterized by long periods of crying, during which your baby is virtually inconsolable. It disrupts naps as well as night-time sleep. As it often strikes in the evening, it can interfere with the bedtime routine.

The origin and nature of colic are uncertain. It may be that the underdeveloped stomach is under strain, that daytime stress is being released, or that the act of crying results in the intake of air into the stomach, with consequent discomfort.

The symptoms can also be quite vague, so it is not always easy to determine whether or not your crying baby is suffering from an episode of colic, particularly if she is generally sensitive and demanding. However,

Limiting the effects of reflux

- Give your baby frequent small feeds or meals, rather than fewer, larger ones.

- Hold your baby upright for 30–60 minutes after a feed and wait for her to bring up wind and regurgitate if necessary. Similarly, allow enough time between her bedtime feed and settling her for the night for this to happen. This will have the added benefit that your baby is not being fed to sleep.

- Elevate your baby's head in her crib or cot; you can place books under the head of the mattress.

- Don't let her cry for too long because this can encourage more food to regurgitate.

- If you are bottle-feeding, experiment with different styles of bottle and teat to help reduce excess air intake during feeding.

- Avoid exposing your baby to cigarette smoke.

Try various holding positions to see which brings most relief to a baby with colic.

if she pulls her legs up in discomfort as she cries or has a distended stomach, or both, you can be fairly certain that she is having an attack of colic.

Unfortunately, this may not help you to relieve it, as there is no known cure for colic and it is often only time that brings relief. Remedies that help some babies may not help others at all. Rhythmic movement, such as rocking and walking around, often helps. Gently rubbing her abdomen or patting her back while holding her across your forearm or up against your shoulder may relieve some of the discomfort. Often, trying to do something is less stressful than doing nothing. Once the episode has run its course, she is likely to be tired and ready to sleep. Nevertheless, it can be extremely wearing for you and this is a time when you would be justified in calling on some respite help from family and friends.

One consolation is that colic rarely lasts beyond 3–4 months of age. However, the sleep problems caused by the colic can easily become habitual. Colicky babies often go on to rely on sleep associations that they pick up during the period of colic, such as being held and rocked to sleep. If this happens, you need to teach your baby new, appropriate sleep associations as the episodes of colic subside (see page 53, Inappropriate sleep associations).

Gastro-oesophageal reflux This is when a baby partially regurgitates her food. This can create stomach pains rather like heartburn, and these will be more uncomfortable when she is lying down. This makes it hard for her to fall asleep and stay asleep. From a medical point of view, this is not a problem as long as your baby is gaining weight and is otherwise healthy, but it can badly disrupt sleep.

Reflux is often caused by immaturity of the digestive system, and almost all babies outgrow it. However, as with colic, don't wait for the symptoms to pass before introducing your baby's bedtime routine, which will help your child to learn good sleep habits.

Milk intolerance

Studies indicate that 5–10 per cent of children have some degree of cow's milk intolerance. The severity of this varies widely, with symptoms ranging from mild stomach pain to breathing difficulties, but all have the potential to disrupt sleep. There are three forms of this condition:

1 **Milk protein allergy** is a true allergy that causes severe symptoms and can only be cured by the complete exclusion of cow's milk and its products from your child's diet. It may be detected with a skin test.

2 **Milk protein intolerance** is not a true allergy but will produce symptoms. However, your child may still be able to have some cow's milk and milk products in her diet.

3 **Lactose intolerance** is caused by a deficiency or absence of lactase – the enzyme that digests milk. This results in undigested milk sugar, or lactose, passing into the colon

A baby suffering from milk intolerance may need winding.

causing bloating and diarrhoea. This can often be remedied with a low-lactose diet.

The symptoms of milk allergy or intolerance are many and varied. They include persistent crying, failure to gain weight, reflux, vomiting, colic, flatulence, bloating, diarrhoea, bowel problems, skin disorders and respiratory problems.

The sheer variety of these symptoms means that you may not suspect a milk intolerance at first, or you may lack proof that this is the cause. In this case, you should seek a medical diagnosis. Your doctor or health visitor will also be able to advise you on what products to avoid and on suitable nutritional substitutes.

Tooth-grinding

Although many adults grind their teeth while asleep, the problem is more common in children. However, while in adults it is usually a sign of stress, in children it is often just a developmental habit that will pass.

Tooth-grinding seems to run in families, occurring equally among boys and girls. Not surprisingly, it is more common in children with minor abnormalities of the teeth.

The child will grind his upper and lower teeth together, usually in bursts of 5–15 seconds. Although this can make quite an audible noise, it does not usually cause problems unless it goes on over a long period. In the short term, it can cause pain in the facial muscles and headaches, which can interfere with napping and night-time sleep. In the longer term, it can result in abnormal wear of the teeth.

Tooth-grinding can be associated with stress and anxiety, so if the problem does not resolve, you need to see a doctor.

There are some steps you can take to discourage or alleviate the causes:

● Ask your dentist for a tooth guard, to protect your child's teeth against abnormal or excessive wear.

● If you think stress anxiety is a factor, first talk to your child about it. The talking alone may help alleviate any worry that may be causing the tooth-grinding.

A diet that is high in fibre can help to alleviate constipation.

Constipation

This will affect most children at some time in their childhood. It has no single identifiable cause, but insufficient fluid or fibre intake is usually a contributory factor. High consumption of otherwise healthy but energy-dense and low-fibre foods, such as cheese, yogurt and bananas, is also a common cause.

The discomfort caused in the lower abdomen is likely to disturb the child's sleep, but only until she is able to empty her bowel.

It is best to try dietary modification before considering medication. This means increasing the child's intake of water and high-fibre foods, such as fruit and vegetables and unrefined cereal products. If this does not work within a couple of days, you can consult your doctor or pharmacist.

Middle ear infection

Ear infections are extremely common in children. They are not always easy to spot and often cause disruption to sleep.

An acute ear infection will be very evident, with symptoms including fever and vomiting as well as ear pain. By contrast, milder chronic middle ear infection, which is caused by a build-up of fluid in the ear, has much more vague symptoms. It can still disturb the child's sleep, although it is not always clear why.

If your child has a history of recurrent ear infections, it is worth checking with your doctor to make sure there is not a build-up of fluid in the middle ear as a result. If this is the case, it can be treated, after which the associated sleep problem should disappear.

Try to reduce your child's fluid intake as night-time approaches.

Bed-wetting

It is common for children to go through a period of wetting the bed when they stop using nappies at night. It is part of the transition to nocturnal bladder control, and typically happens between the ages of 3 and 4 years. However, children differ a lot in their ability to do this, as it is a complex process that involves several developmental advances.

The urinary system has to develop the ability to produce less urine at night, so that the bladder fills less quickly. Coordination has to develop between the maturing nerves and the muscles controlling the bladder. Also, the child has to learn to wake up when her bladder is full. Although all this can happen quite quickly in some children, it typically takes several months.

By the age of 2½ years, most children are dry during the day and, by 3 years old, three-quarters of these are also dry most nights. However, for a lot of children, this is a slow learning process. Boys tend to be slower than girls. By the age of 4 years, 1 in every 10 children still wets the bed at least once a week. The older the child, the more anxiety bed-wetting tends to cause. This should be treated with patience and reassurance but also some practical support (see Box, How you can help).

There is very little scientific evidence to back up the idea that bed-wetting is a psychological problem. Some children wet the bed if they have anxieties at home or school, but bed-wetting is more often a cause, rather than a result, of unhappiness.

It is not uncommon for parents to get cross with a child who continually wets the bed, not least because they will be woken in the night. Try to be patient because any anxiety your child feels about wetting the bed may spill over into other aspects of her sleep behaviour.

Reasons for bed-wetting There are a number of reasons for bed-wetting.

- Genetic susceptibility to bed-wetting runs in families. If one parent had this problem, the likelihood of a child wetting the bed is 40 per cent. This increases to 70 per cent if both parents had the problem.

- The child may just be slightly slow in developing the necessary connections between the nerves and the muscles of the bladder, so that the bladder still empties when it is only half full.

- Some children produce a lot of urine at night because the mechanisms that reduce urine production at night are slow to develop.

- Occasionally, a medical condition, such as a urine infection, is responsible. See your doctor if you suspect this to be the case.

- Children who do not drink much in the early part of the day tend to compensate by drinking a lot in the evening and are then unable to retain the volume of fluid. If your child is at nursery or school, ask the teacher to encourage him to drink more fluids in the earlier part of the day.

How you can help

- Encourage your child to have at least six drinks during the day. This helps to train the bladder to hold larger quantities and will prevent excessive drinking in the evening.

- Restrict caffeinated drinks, such as cola, tea and coffee, as they contain caffeine which can irritate the bladder.

- Lift your child on to the lavatory and encourage her to pass some urine before you go to bed (for instance, at about 11.00 pm). This will not in itself prevent a wet bed, but it will slightly reduce the amount of urine that is released.

- Don't restrict drinks in the evening. If your child seems to want a lot of liquid in the evening, it is probably because she is not drinking enough in the day. The best approach then is to encourage daytime drinking.

- Consider offering a reward to older children when they do not bed-wet to increase their motivation.

Why sleep problems seem difficult

We have all gazed lovingly at our babies or children sleeping – and not just out of relief that at last they are giving us a break. They do it so beautifully and naturally. From their very early days, when they sleep for 16 hours out of every 24, they appear to claim it as their birthright.

Most babies and toddlers can sleep under the most hostile conditions: in a crowded or draughty room, in a buggy bumping over cobblestones, or waiting at the bus stop next to the noisy roadworks. Young children seem able to do this whatever the situation. The innate capacity to sleep against the odds that babies and toddlers demonstrate daily, however, can be deceptive.

As with any other feature of their lives, their sleep patterns change and develop, often rapidly. Just when you have become accustomed to your baby sleeping for 4 hours between feeds and waking twice a night, she will switch to 3 hours, or 5 hours, and wake twice as often. Your toddler will be napping conveniently after lunch for 2 hours and then suddenly start wanting that nap just before tea. She appears to be playing with your well-considered ideas and expectations.

Adapting to such changes is all part of the parenting challenge. It serves to keep us alert to our baby's needs so that we respond quickly and sensitively. Nevertheless, it can be confusing. Often, the abrupt changes we experience in an infant's sleep behaviour are a perfectly normal response, conditioned by her current age, stage of development and temperament (see page 16, What is normal sleep?). The trick is to distinguish these natural transformations from a genuine sleep problem.

To do this, you need to be alert to the changes in your child's sleep behaviour as they evolve. If you anticipate them, it will be easier to differentiate

Spot the sleep problem!

Your child has a sleep problem if she:

- often wakes in the night and calls out to you

- has a bedtime that is getting later over a short period

- regularly comes into your bed in the night

- is feeding at night after 6 months

- wakes up very early several times a week

- is awake for long periods at night

- often puts up a fight at bedtime, refusing to go to bed or settle

- won't go to sleep unless certain conditions are met

- is a young baby and won't sleep in the day

- keeps coming downstairs after being tucked in.

Your child has a sleep problem if she is regularly coming into your bed in the night.

between a natural, healthy change and an emerging problem (see Box). If there is a problem, you will then be able to take steps to manage it at an early stage.

It can seem perverse to interfere in behaviours that have evolved so naturally, especially in a young baby, but remind yourself that it is almost always in the baby's longer-term interest.

What next?

Acknowledging that your child has a sleep problem is a big step. Next is the big leap – doing something about it. Before you embrace that challenge, you need to have some idea of how you are going to approach the problem.

Not knowing where to seek help can hinder even the most inquisitive or assertive parent. But, once you start to enquire, you will find plenty of advice. But whose advice should you take? Your doctor's advice to stop your toddler napping so she will sleep at night conflicts with your mother-in-law's advice to make her sleep at midday on the dot, even if she has to cry for a long time, which conflicts with your partner's advice not to let your baby associate going to sleep with unhappiness and to let her sleep when and where she wants to sleep.

All this advice may well be offered in good faith and, on the surface, sound rational. However, the conflicting messages are disorienting at a time when, with all the other challenges facing you, you need above all simplicity and clarity.

This is exactly what parents have come to us for and what we hope you will find in these pages. Remember that there is not necessarily a single solution for everybody and any solution should be adapted to the family and its circumstances rather than the other way around.

Your sleep matters too

As individuals, babies and children exhibit sleep problems in different ways and at different times, but they all have the same consequence: they make the parents tired. And, as we all know, it is harder to deal with any problem when we are tired.

In fact, if you have turned to this page because you are in the middle of a sleep problem, 'tired' will seem like an insulting understatement. You are completely shattered, and a shattered parent rarely feels ready to take on a new challenge like changing a child's behaviour against her will.

This fatigue displays itself in a range of ways with different people (see page 66, Looking after yourself) and the symptoms can be overwhelming. In addition, recent studies have shown an association between insomnia and health problems as diverse as infertility and obesity. Thus, while helping your child sleep, attending to your own sleep will help both of you.

Looking after yourself

If you want to teach your child to sleep successfully, your primary focus is clearly on your child, but both the problem and its solution can be challenging for you to deal with. Solving a sleep problem is almost always demanding and often frustrating, yet it hits you when you are at a low ebb. You are probably more tired than you have ever been.

For many of us, parenthood is our first encounter with sleep deprivation. Only then can you appreciate why it is successfully used as a form of torture!

Parental sleep deprivation is clearly of a different order and is not an acute or dangerous condition. But it can manifest itself in many insidious ways.

For you, it may lead to a predictable doziness in the late morning, which you treat with large quantities of coffee; an afternoon slump in physical energy and concentration; or irritability that brings you close to tears in the evening. None of these are compatible with the demands of looking after a baby or toddler.

Tiredness may affect your mind as well as body, and almost all parents find it impairs their judgement and makes them impatient. Those who are deprived of REM sleep (see page 18) in particular may find themselves becoming depressed and disorganized.

When REM deprivation affects mothers, the symptoms are often confused with postnatal depression. Most REM sleep occurs in the second half of the night, so if you have a baby or child who regularly wakes early, try to get your partner to do the morning shift for a spell to see if it can help you overcome your sleep deprivation.

Protecting your rest

Although adults are better able than children to cope with sleep deprivation on a day-to-day basis, if it goes on for long they also get run down. It will be no surprise to parents who have had their sleep broken repeatedly that numerous surveys have shown that sleep deprivation can lead to an array of social and physiological problems. These include difficulties at work, marital break-ups and even domestic violence.

Patience, confident decision-making and clarity of purpose are, of course, all very useful when dealing with a sleep problem, but don't wait for them to return spontaneously before doing something about it.

As the child's sleep problem persists unresolved, you will only find your impatience and lack of resolve getting worse.

You need to make sure you get your rest and time off as well. The principle of 'the more you sleep, the better you sleep' applies to adults as well as children.

Some sleep-training methods, such as controlled crying, require a 'now or never' approach and sometimes a steely nerve. Therefore they will be easier if you prepare yourself for action by taking steps to minimize the stresses and demands on yourself.

Survival strategies

The first thing is to engage the support and understanding of your partner. Just talking it through can help; engaging his or her practical support is even better. If you are the one who is bearing the brunt of the broken nights, persuade your partner that he or she will benefit because you will be much better company if you are not dog-tired and grumpy every evening and weekend!

- If your baby's napping schedule is not problematic, try to take an afternoon nap with him.

- When you are feeling the tension of real fatigue and of the day's demands stretching ahead, try to avoid the caffeine-and-biscuits option, which will only give you a temporary lift. Instead, try structured relaxation techniques, such as meditation or yoga, for longer-lasting relief.

- Arrange a night-shift system with your partner if your baby is waking a lot in the night, so that you only get up once. If you are breast-feeding and you think a feed may

Discussing your problems with other mothers can be a great comfort to you: they may even be able to help.

be necessary, express some milk for your partner to use. Swap shifts, so that you both benefit from the different stages of sleep, particularly REM sleep, which comes in the second half of the night.

- If you are bottle-feeding, have a vacuum flask of sterilized hot water and some pre-measured powder ready beside your bed to make up your baby's night-time bottle.

- Accept all offers of help from friends and relatives. Having an older child picked up from school and taken out for tea, for example, can leave you with the extra energy for dealing with night waking.

- If you are so tired or tense that you have problems falling asleep at night, try some natural remedies, such as lavender oil, a hop pillow or camomile tea.

- Go along to a support group for new parents, where you should find a sympathetic ear and some useful tips.

- If you really feel that you are not coping, contact your health visitor or doctor.

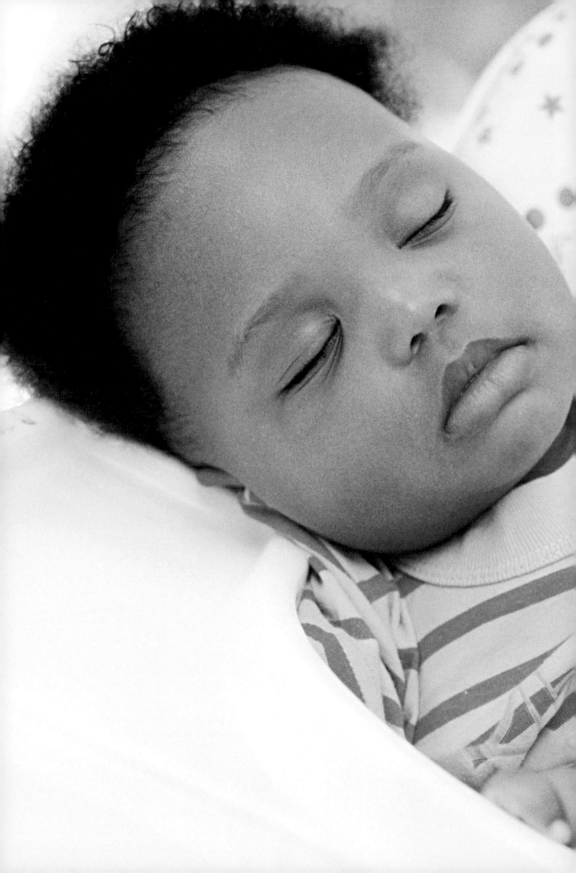

4 Tackling sleep problems

10 key questions – assessing your child's problem

You probably know what your child's sleep problem is, but, before you explore ways of tackling it, it is useful to consider some basic questions about the precise scale and nature of the problem. This will help you to isolate the issues that are causing the problem and, together with the information from your diary (see page 72), will set you on target to sort it out.

1 **Is your child well?** Could your child's sleep disturbance be the result of an illness? An inability to sleep properly can be the first sign of, for example, an ear infection. If so, the priority is to treat the medical condition, but it is also important to ensure that the short-term sleep disturbances do not become longer-term problems. The best way to do this is to maintain as good a sleep routine as possible during the illness, so that it can readily be reinforced when your child is better.

2 **How long has the problem been going on?** Consider whether your child's problems existed from birth or began more recently. If they are of recent origin, were they triggered by a particular event or episode in his life and the family's life? Or are they linked to stages in his development (see page 20), sudden changes in your child's circumstances (see page 44, Times of change) or changes in his sleep routines?

3 **How much sleep does your child get?** Do you know if he is getting enough sleep, both in the daytime and at night? Sleep problems are so disorienting that it can be difficult to remember exactly what has happened in the preceding days and weeks. Completing a sleep diary can help fill this gap, providing a clear picture of

A baby is more likely to sleep at night if daytime naps are consistent.

what is going on (see page 72, Keeping a sleep diary). You can then compare this with normal expectations for a child of his age (see page 16, What is normal sleep?).

4 **How easily does he settle at night?** The bedtime routine often sets the pattern for the night. Is he taking too long to settle? And has he acquired inappropriate sleep associations (see page 53)? He should be settled in his own room and fall asleep alone within 15 minutes of lights out.

5 **Does your child have regular sleep routines?** Irregular routines often underpin sleep problems. Are his nap times and bedtime routine consistent day to day? Again, with the aid of a sleep diary (see page 72), you can identify whether his sleeping and waking times are regular. Establishing appropriate and consistent routines, if these are not already in place, is often the only measure you have to take to solve your child's problem.

6 **Is night waking an issue?** Night waking is a very common sleep problem, but understanding why it happens is the key to solving it. How often does he wake, for how long and for what apparent reason, if any? Check on the normal expectations for a child of his age (see page 16).

What does it take to get him back to sleep? Your response to his night waking is crucial to whether the waking continues or disappears.

7 **Does your child experience sleep-related anxiety?** Anxieties can prevent children settling well. They can be about a whole range of things, although fear of the dark is probably the most common and can contribute to a sleep problem (see page 36, Creating the right environment).

Is your child fearful if awake in the night and are you able to calm or reassure him? Alternatively, are his anxieties caused by other sources of stress that have then resulted in sleep problems?

Does your child thrash around or call out in his sleep? Does he sleep-talk or sleep-walk (see page 54, Sleep disturbances)?

8 **What is your child's condition like in the day?** Sleep problems often have an impact on daytime mood and behaviour – and not just for the child! Is your child sleepy when he gets up, or later in the day? What is his general mood? Does he get irritable or have problems concentrating on what he is doing?

All these can be signs of sleep deprivation arising from sleep disruption or inappropriate sleep times. The sooner you tackle these, the easier their solution.

9 **Is the environment conducive to good sleep?** All kinds of changes in the family can potentially disturb a child's sleep patterns (see page 44, Times of change). These may be unavoidable in the short term, but should not be allowed to become ingrained problems.

The physical environment in which he sleeps is also important. Are the circumstances surrounding his bedtime routine calming? Consider temperature, noise, lights and the behaviour of siblings. Is sharing a room with a sibling exacerbating his difficulties (see Chapter 2, Encouraging good sleep habits)?

10 **What solutions have you previously tried?** Consider any techniques that you have tried before, how long you kept to your plan and to what extent they worked.

Do not assume that a technique that you have already tried will not work ever. Its success may depend greatly on how and when you apply it.

See also flow charts in Chapter 5, Identifying the problem.

Keeping a sleep diary

When does your baby or child sleep and for how long? What influences or interferes with her pattern of sleep? Is the pattern repeated over successive days or weeks?

These are very simple questions but many parents would have difficulty answering them with any certainty. It is not easy to keep mental track of details like this when you are busy and over-tired.

However, in order to establish whether your child has a sleep problem and the kind of treatment it requires, you need this basic information. One of the best ways to collect and record this is to keep a sleep diary.

Like the example, this can be a very simple document, but the crude data that it provides can be used to a variety of ends. A diary:

- Enables you to assess whether your child is getting enough sleep in total and whether sleep is occurring at the best times.

- Helps you to track the progress of any changes you are implementing in your child's day-to-day routine to improve her sleep. Whether you are introducing a full structured sleep programme or just making small initial changes to, say, meal and nap times, you will be better able to ascertain the impact of what you are doing.

- Helps you to be more objective and open about a problem that is often emotionally charged. With the bare facts in front of you, it is much easier to spot the emergence of any specific patterns, which you can then address quickly before they cause greater difficulties.

Millpond sleep diary – age 9 months

1 Early rising contributes to multiple naps in the day

2 First nap too early; treated by baby as night sleep

3 Midday nap too early and too short; needs extra nap that is taken too close to bedtime

4 Three naps is one too many at this age

5 First light sleep phase – usually no need to respond

	MONDAY	TUESDAY	WEDNESDAY
Time woke in morning	5.30 am ❶	6.00 am	6.10 am
Time and length of nap(s) in day	7.00–10.30 am ❷ 12.00–1.00 pm ❸ 4.00–5.00 pm ❹	7.30–7.45 am ❷ 12.00–1.00 pm ❸ 4.00–4.30 pm ❹	9.00–9.45 am ⓫ 1.30–3.00 pm
Time start prep. for bed in evening	6.00 pm	6.00 pm ❼	6.00 pm
Time went to bed in evening	7.00 pm	7.15 pm	7.00 pm
Time went to sleep	8.00 pm ❿	8.30 pm ❿	7.15 pm
Time(s) woke in the night; what you did; time(s) went to sleep again	10.30/11.00 pm brought into parents' bed ❺ 2.00–2.45 am feed ❻ 4.30–5.00 am feed ⓬	11.00 pm cuddled and put back into own bed ❺ ❽ 3.00 am feed ⓬	10.00–11.00 pm cuddled and put back into own bed ❺ ❽ 2.00 am feed 4.30 am fed and brought into parents' bed ⓬

- Enables you to see the connections between what your child is doing outside sleep times and the way this affects her sleep.

- Throws light on your responses to your child's sleep habits, enabling you to see where your are genuinely helping or unintentionally hindering the problem.

- Provides you with baseline information against which you can assess not only changes in your child's behaviour but also your management of those changes.

- Helps you to behave consistently, which is especially important when trying to establish a routine.

- Enables any health professional that you consult to advise more readily on an appropriate course of action for you to undertake with your child.

- Can substantially increase your motivation by revealing small improvements in your child's sleeping habits when you have changed her routine.

You may also like to make a note of your key aim at the bottom of the diary page. Rather like a corporate mission statement, this can keep you focused on your goal when messy day-to-day business gets in the way, clouds your judgement and threatens to throw you off course.

When is the best time to start keeping a diary? The answer is almost certainly today. Even if you have not yet decided how to tackle your child's sleep problem, any information you gather now will give you a head start in determining which approach to take and subsequently how you are progressing.

You may be surprised what a simple daily diary can teach you, and this knowledge will help you teach your child to sleep.

THURSDAY	FRIDAY	SATURDAY	SUNDAY
6.20 am	7.30 am	6.00 am	7.00 am
9.30–10.15 am 1.00–2.00 pm **9** 4.30–6.00 pm **4**	10.00–10.45 am **11** 1.30–3.00 pm	9.30–10.15 am **11** 1.30–3.00 pm	10.15–11.30 am **11** 2.00–3.30 pm
7.30 pm	6.15 pm	6.00 pm	6.15 pm
8.30 pm	7.15 pm	7.00 pm	7.15 pm
9.30 pm **10**	7.30 pm	7.30 pm	7.30 pm
12.15–12.30 am cuddled and put back to **8** own bed 4.00 am fed and put back **12** in own bed	3.00–3.30 am fed and put back in **12** own bed	11.00 pm–12.30 am cuddled, wouldn't go back to **8** sleep; eventually came into parents' bed 4.30 am fed and stayed in **12** parents' bed	4.30 am fed and put back in own **12** bed; slept to morning

6 More difficult to get baby back to sleep in early hours

7 Starting bedtime routine too early compared with natural sleep time: 1 hour is plenty

8 Rewards for waking

9 Having third nap late then not ready to sleep at bedtime

10 Long gap between going to bed and falling asleep – should be more like 15 minutes

11 Better timed naps and woke later – whole day flows better

12 Inappropriate night feeds – none necessary at 9 months

Sleep-training techniques

Most sleep problems require decisive and consistent action in order to remedy them, and few parents can do this intuitively. Most need a technique that will provide them with a code of management to follow until they see results and a point of reference for when things go wrong.

In the next few pages, we explain the most tried-and-tested techniques. Which you choose will be a personal decision, based on a number of factors: your child's sleep problem; your parenting style; your living conditions and your family composition.

To help you identify the nature of the problem you are experiencing and pinpoint the best technique and direction for you to follow, refer to the relevant flow charts in Chapter 5 (Identifying the problem) and, to see how they work in action, refer to the appropriate case studies in Chapter 6 (Sleep solutions).

Remember that, with all these techniques, the problem is likely to get worse before it gets better. Although there is often a 'honeymoon' period at the beginning, this is frequently followed by a 'test night' or two, when your child will often rebel – but

persistence always pays off. Be prepared for less sleep at first, in the knowledge that the time and energy you invest will produce long-term benefits.

All these techniques work best if both parents are fully committed to them and are ready to provide mutual support. They also depend on a regular and relaxing bedtime routine (see page 30, Creating a sleep routine and page 48, Dos and don'ts).

Night-feed weaning

Babies and toddlers who are fed to sleep, whether by breast or bottle, often demand milk when they wake in the night as a prerequisite to going back to sleep. This does not, however, necessarily mean that they are hungry. They have simply learned a habit, which can be readily changed (see page 87, What if...?).

Babies have less incentive to wake at night if there is little chance of a feed.

Schedule for reducing or spacing feeds

	Reducing the volume of the feed		Increasing the interval between feeds
	Fluid ounces (ml) in each bottle	Minutes breast-feeding	Hours between feeds
Day 1	7.5 (225)	7.5	2
Day 2	7 (210)	7	
Day 3	6.5 (195)	6.5	2.5
Day 4	6 (180)	6	
Day 5	5.5 (165)	5.5	3
Day 6	5 (150)	5	
Day 7	4.5 (135)	4.5	3.5
Day 8	4 (120)	4	
Day 9	3.5 (105)	3.5	4
Day 10	3 (90)	3	
Day 11	2.5 (75)	2.5	4.5
Day 12	2 (60)	2	
Day 13	1.5 (45)	1.5	5
Day 14	1 (30)	1	
Day 15	0.5 (15)	0.5	
Day 16	0		0

Note: If you prefer you can reduce the amount of milk by 1 fl oz (30 ml) or 1 minute breast-feeding each night. This will shorten the process.

Method You don't have to wean your baby completely in order to stop night feeding. You simply have to break the association between feeding and falling asleep, so that he feeds only in the day. The best way to do this is to reduce the frequency of the night-time feeds or to reduce the amount of milk given on each waking. You don't need to do both.

Your baby will gradually wake less for milk and eventually give it up altogether. However, feeds should not be eliminated in a baby under 6 months old, as most babies require night feeding for energy and good nutrition until this age. For babies of this age who are feeding too frequently in the night, you therefore need to space the feeds rather than reduce them (see Table).

If your baby has trouble going back to sleep while spacing or reducing feeds you may need to incorporate a sleep technique to resettle him.

See also pages 138–147, Solutions 13–17

Controlled crying

Controlled crying is a sleep-training method that teaches your child to fall asleep independently. Your child is not left abandoned to his tears, as you return to briefly check on him at set intervals, increasing the time between visits until he goes to sleep.

Method After following your bedtime routine, place your child in his cot awake and leave the room. Return after 5 minutes to briefly check your child. This is not to ease or stop the crying, or to get him back to sleep, but simply to reassure him that you are there and to check that he is well.

You should not go right up to your baby or toddler, just tell him sympathetically but firmly to go to sleep and that you will see him in the morning. The key to this technique is not to cuddle, pat or pick him up.

The idea is to increase the interval between visits by 5 minutes each time, starting with 5 minutes and going up to a maximum of 15 minutes. If your child continues to cry vigorously keep checking him until he goes to sleep. A minority of children may be over-stimulated by frequent visits, resulting in prolonged waking. If you think this is the case, start your initial check after 10 minutes and increase this interval to a maximum of 20 minutes (see Table on page 76).

If you apply the rule properly, your child should not cry for much more than an hour – but be prepared for more, just in case. Repeat the procedure every time the child wakes in the night – starting at the minimum waiting time and building up to the maximum until waking up time in the morning. Apply this same proceedure to daytime naps.

Checking on your child		
First check	Second check	Third and subsequent checks (until asleep)
5 minutes	10 minutes	15 minutes

During what can be a gruelling few nights, it is worth reminding yourself of three things: the crying will not cause your baby or toddler any psychological damage. The considerable benefits to him – and you – of improved sleep will outweigh his temporary discomfort; and it is almost certainly harder on you than on your child.

Advantages

- This is usually the quickest sleep-training method: you can expect your child to start to sleep through the night within as little as 7–10 days.

- This is the most unambiguous technique, leaving you in no doubt as to what you need to do and how to do it.

- It is one of the easiest techniques to reapply after minor disruptions to sleep patterns.

Disadvantages

- It can be emotionally challenging and wearing, as parents find it counter-intuitive to leave a child to cry for long periods.

- On rare occasions, a child may cry so much that he vomits. This can be distressing for the parents but is unlikely to happen more than once or twice.

- This method is not usually adopted for babies aged under about 6 months or for children aged 3 years and over.

- This method is inappropriate for children with anxiety problems.

See also page 86, What if...? and page 124, Solution 6

Gradual retreat

This military-sounding technique is one of the more gentle, based on the idea of the parents distancing themselves from the child little by little until the child no longer requires their presence to fall asleep. This more gradual approach gives the child time to adjust to the ever-increasing distances.

Method Parents adopt different degrees of physical closeness in order to help their child get to sleep. These include:

- lying down with the child

- sitting on the edge of the bed

- sitting on a chair next to his bed

- being across the room, just to be seen.

The aim of gradual retreat is to move on to the next degree of physical separation. For example, if you normally sit on your child's bed, your first step is to move to a bedside chair. Maintain this position for 3 nights. You can take the next step, which is to move the chair further away from the bed. Continue to move further away until, finally, you are outside your child's room.

For this programme to be effective it is important to observe the following guidelines.

1 Resist your child's protests and pleas to return to your previous position.

2 Plan your route out of the room so you know your next move. This will also give you an idea of how long the process will take – the smaller the bedroom, the smaller the moves!

3 Repeat each step for 3 nights before moving

on to the next stage. Keep going until you are just inside the door of the bedroom – usually 7–10 days later – then move outside the door. Moving outside the door can be the hardest step in a gradual retreat programme.

4 Do not interact with your child while you are sitting in his room. You are not there to be an audience or to pay attention to any inappropriate behaviour. Make minimal eye contact and limit all conversations to basic commands, such as: 'Oliver, lie down and go to sleep' (see page 86, What if...?).

5 Make sure your child is fully asleep before leaving his room. Wait an extra 10 minutes to be sure of this. You don't want him to catch you tip-toeing out of the room and have to start the whole process over again.

6 If your child is old enough, introduce a reward system for going to sleep as you distance yourself from him. This will help

to reinforce the progress you have made and will make the experience more positive for your child (see page 82, Positive reinforcement – rewards).

7 If your child also wakes during the night, you should repeat the same process that you followed at bedtime.

8 Keep a sleep diary to monitor the changes and assess your progress (see page 72).

Advantages

- This method involves less crying, so it is less stressful for the parent and, for the same reason, can be used even when the bad sleeper is sharing a room with a sibling.

- It is appropriate for a child of any age.

- It is a good method to use if your child is particularly anxious.

Disadvantages

- It may take up to a month for your child to respond.

- It may be unclear when the problem has been solved and, if you stop prematurely, there is a strong chance of relapse.

- It requires a lot of the parents, who need to be patient and persistent over a sustained period of time.

See also page 97, flow chart 3; and page 120, Solution 4

Simple and gentle in its application, the gradual retreat technique is suitable for a child of any age.

Elimination

A child's inappropriate night-time behaviour is often unintentionally rewarded by their parents. Sometimes this behaviour starts after a break in routine – such as a holiday or a stay with relatives – when parents may have responded to night waking rather than ignoring it.

The technique of elimination is about removing such rewards on the basis that, if the behaviour is ignored rather than rewarded, it will soon cease. For example, a child who comes downstairs in the late evening might get a cuddle on the sofa before going back to bed. In this case, the technique would simply be to send the child straight back to bed without a cuddle.

Rewarding a child's behaviour can inadvertently create inappropriate sleep associations. The 'rewards' that reinforce inappropriate behaviour can be physical, emotional or environmental, and include watching television, hugs, or sympathy or sleeping in the parents' bed. (See page 36, Creating the right environment.)

Method This method is only truly effective if you are sure you have identified the reward that is maintaining the behaviour. This can be difficult as some rewards are very subtle, for example, another kiss when returning to tuck your child back into bed during the night. Once you have identified the reward you will need to decide how to withhold it.

If your child is old enough, state clearly what you require of her and the new 'rules' when you are putting her to bed. Whenever she repeats the behaviour after that, respond by restating your requirements and getting her to comply without the 'reward'. For example, if she gets up and comes into your bed, take her by the hand and lead her back to bed, restating firmly what you expect of her now. Do not enter into complicated explanations or justifications. In applying this technique you must make sure your child is safe when you ignore her behaviour.

Do this consistently each time the behaviour is repeated. Keep to your word kindly but firmly and do not respond to her protests. This will mean ignoring her cries or pleas.

This is simple in principle but not easy in practice: you need to maintain your resolve firmly until your child's behaviour changes. This can be emotionally tough on parents but, if your resolve weakens, you will probably reinforce the behaviour. If you feel unable to tough it out, try one of the more gradual approaches.

For older children, the technique works well in conjunction with a reward system (see page 82).

Advantages

- If you are certain at the onset what reward is maintaining the behaviour and remove it straight away, this technique usually works very quickly.

- This is a good quick-fix technique to use after minor disruptions to the sleep routine, such as holidays or illness.

Disadvantages

- Things often get worse before they improve.

- Parents find that it requires a lot of emotional effort to persevere and resist responding to a child's behaviour.

See also Chapter 2, Encouraging good sleep habits;
page 100, flow chart 5; and page 154,
Solution 21

Eliminating undesirable behaviour

Behaviour	Reward	Elimination
Your child wakes up and keeps calling for you	Attention and a cuddle	Ignore her calls
Your child gets up and comes into your bed	Leave her there while gently telling her that she must go back to bed soon	Get her out of your bed immediately and take her back to her own bed
Your child keeps throwing her dummy out of the cot	Replace her dummy and give her a cuddle	Check on her but do not replace her dummy

Resetting your child's body clock

This technique is specifically designed to deal with the problem of a child who goes to sleep and wakes up too early or who goes to sleep and wakes up too late. These patterns are often called early and late sleep phase.

The method of dealing with this focuses entirely on the timing of sleep, since quality and length of sleep are rarely an issue. The aim is to shift the whole period of night-time sleep forwards or backwards.

The shift is made gradually, so that the child's body clock can accommodate the change; if the changes are made too quickly, she is likely to relapse. Stick rigidly to the new schedule, even at weekends and holidays, until you are certain that the child's body clock has fully adapted.

Early sleep phase – method This mostly affects very young children and is the easiest to deal with. You simply delay the child's bedtime by an extra 10–15 minutes each evening, until you arrive at the desired bedtime (see Table). You may need to move mealtimes and daytime naps accordingly. During this period, do not interfere with wake times, which should adjust themselves as the time of sleep onset is advanced.

Late sleep phase – method Late sleep phase is when a child's natural sleeping time becomes later than is appropriate for her age. Once asleep, she sleeps well and, if left, wakes after a full night's sleep. However, if she has to be woken, for example, to go to school or nursery, she remains sleepy and tired throughout the day. Parents often regard late sleep phase as a bedtime battle or as an inability on the part of the child to fall asleep. An older child may become anxious about bedtime if she feels incapable of going to sleep.

These problems often arise after a holiday, when a child has become accustomed to being allowed to stay up later, or when parents don't keep to a set bedtime and she gradually falls asleep later and later.

There are two strategies (see Table on page 80) for tackling this problem, depending on the circumstances.

- **Plan A** (see page 80) is for the child who needs to make a shift in time of 3 hours or less, and does not yet go to nursery or school. It can also be used during holiday times with children of school age. With this approach, you gradually wake the child earlier and earlier as well as bringing bedtime forward.

- **Plan B** (see page 80) is for the child who has to get up at a set time from Monday to Friday and needs to make a shift of several hours.

Before you embark on either of these plans, keep a sleep diary (see page 72) in order to work out when your child naturally falls asleep and wakes up.

Early sleep phase plan

Period	Bedtime	Waking
Problem sleep phase	05.00 pm	05.00 am
Day 1	05.15 pm	Spontaneous waking
Day 2	05.30 pm	Spontaneous waking
Day 3	05.45 pm	Spontaneous waking
Day 4	06.00 pm	Spontaneous waking
Day 5	06.15 pm	Spontaneous waking
Day 6	06.30 pm	Spontaneous waking
Day 7	06.45 pm	Spontaneous waking
Day 8	07.00 pm	Spontaneous waking
Day 9	07.15 pm	Spontaneous waking
Day 10	07.30 pm	Spontaneous waking
Resulting sleep phase	07.30 pm	06.30 am

Note: Parents **must** start the bedtime routine only 30–40 minutes before actual bedtime.

Late sleep phase plan

Plan A			Plan B		
Period	Bedtime	Waking	Period	Bedtime	Waking
Problem sleep phase	10.00 pm	10.00 am	Problem sleep phase	11.00 pm	07.15 am
Night I	10.00 pm	10.00 am	Night I–3	11.00 pm	07.15 am
Night 2	10.00 pm	10.00 am	Night 4–7	10.45 pm	07.15 am
Night 3	10.00 pm	09.45 am	Night 8–11	10.30 pm	07.15 am
Night 4	10.00 pm	09.30 am	Night 12–15	10.15 pm	07.15 am
Night 5	10.00 pm	09.15 am	Night 16–19	10.00 pm	07.15 am
Night 6	10.00 pm	09.00 am	Night 20–23	09.45 pm	07.15 am
Night 7	09.45 pm	08.45 am	Night 24–27	09.30 pm	07.15 am
Night 8	09.30 pm	08.30 am	Night 28–31	09.15 pm	07.15 am
Night 9	09.15 pm	08.15 am	Night 32–35	09.00 pm	07.15 am
Night 10	09.00 pm	08.00 am	Night 36–39	08.45 pm	07.15 am
Night 11	08.45 pm	08.00 am	Night 40–43	08.30 pm	07.15 am
Night 12	08.30 pm	08.00 am			
Night 13	08.15 pm	08.00 am			
Night 14	08.00 pm	08.00 am			
Resulting sleep phase	08.00 pm	08.00 am	Resulting sleep phase	08.15 pm	07.15 am

Note: With both plans, parents must start the bedtime routine only 30–40 minutes before actual bedtime.

Plan A

Step 1 For the first 3 nights, put your child to bed at the latest average time they naturally fall asleep. Start the bedtime routine only 30–40 minutes before putting him to bed and don't mention bedtime until 10 minutes beforehand. Avoid any bedtime battles and arguments and keep evening activities quiet (see page 48, Dos and don'ts). Monitor how long he takes to fall asleep, which should take no more than 15 minutes. Once he has done this for 3 nights, proceed to step 2.

Step 2 Begin to wake your child 15 minutes earlier each day. Keep the bedtime at the late time you decided in step 1, do this for 3 more nights.

Step 3 Once you are waking your child an hour earlier, usually about a week later, start to bring the bedtime routine and bedtime earlier by 15 minutes each night.

Step 4 When your child reaches the appropriate waking time, keep to it even at holidays and weekends. (Some children's body clocks can be easily upset, even with a lie in at weekends, and the whole problem could start again.)

Step 5 Continue to bring your child's bedtime forward every night until you reach the appropriate time. (To check your child's sleep needs, see page 16.) You may find your child becomes sleep-deprived as you get him up earlier in the morning. Don't let him take extra naps in the day to make up the time. This is a short-term situation, which is why it is best done in holidays if he is of school age. Stick rigidly to the plan and it will work very well.

Plan B
Step 1 See Plan A.

Step 2 After 3 nights of the later bedtime, bring the bedtime routine and bedtime forward by 15 minutes. Always wake your child at the usual time, for example, 7.15 am, even at weekends. Do this for 3 nights.

Step 3 Advance bedtime by 15 minutes for 3 nights.

Step 4 Continue to advance bedtime by 15 minutes every 3 nights until you reach the appropriate time. (To check your child's sleep needs, see page 16.)

Step 5 As you approach your goal, your child may find it increasingly difficult to go to sleep at the desired time. In this case, it may be best to slow down the process and only move the time forward on a weekly basis.

Slow progress is better than no progress. A reward system (see page 82, Positive reinforcement – rewards) can work well if your child is of the appropriate age.

See also page 108, flow chart 9, and page 150, Solution 19

Door-shutting

This works well for toddlers and children who keep getting out of bed at bedtime or wake in the night. The aim is to teach them that they can get back to sleep by themselves without a 'quick fix' from you.

Method When a child gets up in the evening or in the night, put him back into bed and tell him to stay there or you will close the door. If he gets up again, close the door, but only for 1 minute. Repeat this each time he gets up, lengthening the time that the door is shut by 1 minute on each occasion, keeping it closed up to a maximum of 5 minutes on night one (see Table, Door-shutting plan).

If he is in bed, praise him, then leave, but if he is out of bed, repeat the door-shutting technique, leaving the door shut for an increased time as per the plan. In this way, you are giving a message that having the door open is under his control: if he wants it open, he can choose to stay in bed.

The door-shutting technique takes a lot of conscientious effort on the part of the parent, but usually works within 7–10 days. This method also works well in conjunction with a reward system.

See also page 100, flow chart 5; and page 154, Solution 21

Door-shutting plan

Number of minutes to close the door

Period	First-time	Second–	Third–	Fourth–	Fifth–	Subsequent–
Night 1	1	2	3	4	5	5
Night 2	2	3	4	5	6	6
Night 3	3	4	5	6	7	7
Night 4	4	5	6	7	8	8
Night 5	5	6	7	8	9	9
Night 6	6	7	8	9	10	10
Night 7	7	8	9	10	11	11

Positive reinforcement – rewards

The parent who has never offered a reward as an incentive for a resistant child to change her behaviour is a rare being. Most have also worried about crossing that fine line between positive reinforcement and downright bribery. However, if handled correctly, rewards can be beneficial and can work as well for sleep as for any other behavioural problems.

When and how to offer rewards

Rewards will only work if your child understands the concept inherent in reward-giving. This may sound obvious but many parents will, in understandable desperation, try to get their child to agree to a conditional behaviour before they are psychologically ready. The child also needs to be emotionally ready for deferred gratification because the reward will not come until the following day.

The child is usually ready to put the idea of cause and effect, behaviour and reward, into practice by the age of 3 years. You will know if your child has reached this stage when she responds to conditional requests about other issues, such as only having sweets if she brushes her teeth or only getting out another toy if she puts the first away.

What kind of reward?

Rewards fall into three categories: an object, such as a small toy, a chocolate, or something to collect; an activity, such as going on a picnic or to the swings; and a sensory or social reward, such as hugs or special time with parents.

These can all work, and it is wrong to think that a durable object is more effective than, say, a cuddle with extra story time from you. Rewards that capture

Man-made sunrise

Placing a magic lamp in your child's room can work very well for early rising and some night-waking problems. The lamp is used with a timer switch and is set to come on at a given time. Using a low-wattage bulb will prevent the lamp waking your child unnecessarily. Finding the lamp on when she wakes will be her cue to get up, but if it is not on, she should return back to sleep.

Before using this method, note your child's waking times (see page 72, Sleep diary). On the first day, set the lamp to come on 15 minutes before her average waking time, so that it is on when she wakes. This approach works well with a reward system such as the sleep fairy.

Explain to your child that she must stay in bed until the lamp comes on. If she achieves this, the sleep fairy will leave a reward. Then shift the time 15 minutes later every 3 days until the appropriate time is achieved. If your child cannot stay in bed until the lamp is on refer to page 89, What if...? As your child moves closer to her target time, make weekly changes. Slow progress is better than no progress. If you try to force the time change too quickly you may jeopardize the progress you have already made.

a child's imagination, such as the sleep fairy (see below), or that emotionally stimulate her, such as warm praise, are as valuable to a child as an item from the toy shop.

Similarly, if you decide to offer an object, size or price is not a determinant of success. If a child is offered a huge reward, such as a new puppy or a holiday, she may feel overwhelmed by the responsibility and be unable to accept it as a fair exchange. On the other hand, a small treat, such as her favourite cereals for breakfast if she complies with your requests at night, are both more tangible and more manageable.

Setting up and giving a reward

First of all, you need to know that the goal is achievable and the reward will be valued – you can talk to her about this. If you start with an easily achievable goal, you will engage your child, and you can then gradually increase the requirements for getting the reward.

You then need to be very clear about the basic rules. Establish an understanding with your child about what they need to achieve, what the reward will be and when it will be given. It is worth remembering that a younger child's concept of time is still developing, so she will be less able to wait. Immediate rewards will be a greater incentive.

Once a reward has been given, do not withdraw it, whatever the child's behaviour the day after, the reward you have given was for a very specific achievement. If your child begins to lose motivation revisit the reward system but make sure the goals are achievable and the reward is motivating for your child.

Practical rewards that work

The sleep fairy Like the tooth fairy, the sleep fairy is a fictional being who magically comes to the child's house when she is asleep at night and leaves her a reward. Make sure your child understands what she has to achieve to get a reward from the fairy.

The reward is given in a special little box or bag, which is next to your bed. In this way, you, as the fairy's human agent, can put a reward in the box in the morning, when you know whether the child has merited it.

If a child's motivation wanes, or you need to stimulate her imagination more, use your own imagination. A written note from the fairy, or a picture or a little paper star from her wand, can all support the fantasy. Similarly, if your child doesn't respond to fairies, bring in a favourite story character instead.

Star chart

This takes a little setting up and explaining, but can be very effective. As with all reward systems, you need to start with achievable goals. Rewarding children with a star tends to work well from about the age of 4 years, when they may have been exposed to the idea of stars as prizes at nursery or school and when they are ready to understand it. The child is rewarded with a star on a chart for each day that she achieves the behaviour you have requested. Sometimes this alone, combined with verbal praise, is enough. If not, you can promise a small present whenever your child has accumulated a certain number of stars. However, do not give her too many or she may lose interest!

Stopping the system

Once your child has reached the desired goal, it is best to continue the reward system for another month until his sleep pattern is firmly establish.

Stopping the sleep fairy Once the new sleep pattern is firmly established you can begin to stop the reward system.

Make a point of not putting out a reward one night and explain to your child that the sleep fairy was visiting other children that night.

She can visit the following night but gradually increase the number of nights when she is 'too busy' until you can stop her visits completely. You could leave a note from the fairy on the final night saying 'Well done! Keep trying hard'.

Stopping the star chart Gradually 'forget' to offer stars. If your child reminds you, apologize for your bad memory and continue to offer stars for the next few nights before 'forgetting' again. Even though you stop offering stars, continue to praise and recognize your child's progress.

What if ...?

While a well-planned and well-implemented programme has a very good chance of success, there are obviously sometimes glitches and setbacks on the way. Below are answers to some of the common 'What if?' questions parents raise. Some of these are general, in that they can apply to many situations. Others are related to particular circumstances or techniques described elsewhere in this book.

General problems

What if my baby stands up in the cot?
This tends to happen towards the end of the baby's first year as she gains mobility. Problems arise if the baby cannot lower herself back down and has to wait for someone to do so before she falls and hurts herself. Once resettled by her parent, often she will get back up again, which can be frustrating.

During the daytime, teach your baby to lower herself from a standing position by practising pulling-up and sitting-back-down games.

Until your baby has learned to lower herself, go in and sit or lay her down, but keep interaction to a minimum because too much attention may cause her to continue the behaviour.

As soon as you are confident that your baby can lower herself safely, you do not need to go to her when she stands up.

What if my baby rolls over and is unable to sleep in this position?
From around 5–6 months your baby will begin to roll back to front. Until he is able to reposition himself freely you will need to put him in the 'back to sleep' position for safety reasons (see page 38, Safe sleeping).

Whatever you do, keep night-time interaction to a minimum. In the day, use lots of floor play to encourage rolling, but recognize that it is very difficult to speed up the natural development process.

A baby sleeping bag may help a restless baby.

What if my baby loses her dummy?
A baby that often loses her dummy at night will more than likely need you to replace it at some stage so that she can return to sleep.

Once your baby can stand in her cot, make sure she cannot harm herself if she falls.

If your child is too young to replace the dummy herself, you may have to consider weaning her off this habit. With an older child, you may be able to attach the dummy to her nightclothes with a special clip and encourage her to replace it herself. Putting another couple of dummies in the bed for her to find is another solution.

It is even better to teach your child a new association for going to sleep and to gradually wean her off a dummy altogether. Start this weaning process by giving your child a dummy less and less often during the day, to reduce her dependency on it. Then, as you gain more confidence, use the same approach at night. To achieve this, you may need to use one of the sleep techniques explained earlier, such as gradual retreat (see page 76) or controlled crying (see page 75).

What if my toddler jumps out of his cot?

Try lowering his mattress so that he cannot physically climb out and he will probably give up trying. Also, remove all objects from his cot so that he cannot gain any leverage to push himself out.

Don't reward him for climbing out, for example by taking him into your bed. Be firm. Try to catch him early. Go into his room and say 'No' firmly. If you do this consistently, he will probably stop trying.

If all this fails, and your child does not stop getting out despite your efforts, transfer him to a bed. You may have to use a stair gate to restrict night-time mobility and avoid accidents, as well as making sure that his room is safe.

What if my child keeps asking for 'just one more' ?

Many children are skilled in asking for 'just one more', whatever it is. A child should always get one chance: she may genuinely need help with her blankets, or a drink of water or a trip to the toilet. Responding once will give her confidence that you are there if needed.

After that, be firm. Tell her to 'Go to sleep' and repeat this as necessary. But when you say 'This is the last time I tell you,' make sure you mean it.

Stay calm. Often children will think that negative attention is better than no attention at all! Children will test the rules but, once they know how far they can go, they will stop.

What if my child sneaks into our bed without us knowing?

Work out a way of alerting yourself whenever he comes into the room. For example:

- Hang something on the back of your door that will 'clang' when the door is opened, such as a kitchen ladle or a fish slice.

- Put a chair inside your bedroom door so that the door will bang against it if opened.

- Put a stair gate across the bedroom door.

- Put a bell on your child's bedroom door so that it rings if he opens his door.

In this way, you can take or send your child back to his bed every time he comes to your room – be consistent with this.

Illness

What if my child is ill?

When your child is ill, you must do whatever is required to help her get better and consult your doctor if necessary. However, you should also try to avoid 'going backwards' as regards her sleep habits if at all possible.

Even if you are in the process of applying a sleep programme, do not leave your child to cry if she has a raised temperature. If you need to give medication, do so at the earliest opportunity to avoid discomfort or restless behaviour.

If your child will not settle, try to resist taking her into your bed to comfort her. Instead, keep her in her own bed and tell her you will sit next to her until she is asleep.

If you have stopped feeding your child at night or are in the process of weaning her off night feeds, you don't need to increase her milk intake during the night just because she is unwell. If she is dehydrated, it is better to offer water rather than milk first; your child's appetite will pick up as soon as she is well again.

Above all, go back to your programme of sleep improvement as soon as your child has recovered (see page 47, Illness).

What if my baby is teething?

See page 47, Teething.

Bedtime battles

What if my child refuses pre-bed milk?
More important than your child refusing pre-bed milk is the fact that he learns to fall asleep without a sucking or milk association.

Make sure he eats well during the day and try bringing his teatime forward a little if possible. He may then feel more like taking milk and, after a night or two, will settle into the new routine.

What if my child resists the new routine?
Although it is difficult, try to remain calm and focused. Make sure you are clear and consistent about the new routine, and do not give in to repeated requests or delaying tactics. Be encouraging. After 2–3 nights she will probably accept the changes.

What if my child won't settle if my partner puts him to bed?
Your baby may be dependent on you for feeding or sucking to go to sleep. Having your partner share the bedtime and night-time settling will help to break that dependence and teach your child new associations. Persevere in sharing the task. As long as both parents are consistent with the routine, your child will eventually accept the other parent.

What if my child finds it difficult to relax at bedtime?
Try to find out whether your child has any problems that are causing anxieties, such as difficulties at school or nursery. If so, talk to her about those problems if she is old enough. However, choose a quiet time during the day – not bedtime.

Make sure the hour before preparation for bed is quiet winding-down time. Encourage quiet play and make the bedtime routine relaxing. For an older child, stay with her while she is in the bath rather than catching up on your chores. Try talking about the positive things that have happened during the day and perhaps what good things are in store for tomorrow.

Try a back massage before putting her into her nightclothes. Allow for story time and try to read to her. Even older children who can read themselves perfectly well enjoy being read to.

Controlled crying

What if my child vomits?
This is upsetting for parents but not as upsetting for babies. Simply change his sheets – trying to keep him in his cot if you can – leave the room and continue with the controlled crying. Make his teatime and his pre-bed feed earlier on successive nights until the vomiting stops.

What if I am doing controlled crying and my baby is hysterical?
This usually happens at the beginning of the programme. Try to avoid picking her up or trying to calm her as you will only prolong the waking.

What if my child is still crying after an hour?
You have to persevere. If you give up now you are only teaching your child that crying for an hour will get him the attention that he craves. It will improve the next time he wakes.

Gradual retreat

What if my child keeps getting out of bed and talking or singing?
Be firm and stay calm. You need to reinforce the 'rules' – that she must stay in bed and go to sleep nicely with her parent in the room. Don't fall into the trap of putting her back into bed each time or negotiating – it just becomes a game and you won't win.

You may need to repeatedly leave the room for 10–20 seconds, shutting the door behind you. If the behaviour continues, you could consider using the door-shutting technique (see page 81) until she cooperates. You want to avoid being an audience to this behaviour and reinforcing it by your presence.

What if my child takes a long time to go back to sleep with a parent in the room?
Some children are kept awake by the presence of a parent in the room. You still need to continue to retreat gradually every 2–3 days. It may be that he doesn't go off to sleep quickly until you are finally outside the door.

Be consistent with an inconsolable child: she will settle after the first few anxious nights.

What if my child keeps waking as I leave the bedroom?

Your child has not entered into deep sleep. Wait at least 10 minutes after she has fallen asleep before you leave the room. Some children may take a little longer.

What if my child becomes very anxious and resists my moving away?

Stay calm and be consistent. Once you have moved on, don't feel tempted to move closer to your child. Reassure him that you will stay with him until he is asleep. You may need to devise a reward system to encourage your child to keep up with your moves and to increase his motivation (see page 82, Positive reinforcement – rewards).

What if I feel the whole process is taking too long?

You need to be patient. It usually takes 10–14 days to get out of the room. You must not rush the technique because otherwise it may not work.

What if my baby cries a lot with gradual retreat, even when I am holding him?

Your baby may be irritated by the contact, which he fears may be relinquished at any moment. If this does not settle down within a couple of nights, continue with the retreat programme, moving on to a stage at which he feels more comfortable.

Night feeding

What if I am weaning my baby off night feeds and she suddenly wakes more frequently and seems hungry?

Continue with the weaning programme and your baby's feeding pattern will adjust naturally. Encourage her to feed more in the daytime and slow down the reduction in the amounts of feeds for 2–3 days (see Table on page 74, Night-feed weaning).

What if my baby is teething and not eating in the day. Do I start feeding him again at night?

No. Your baby may need extra fluid if he has a temperature or is dehydrated but he should not need food. As soon as he recovers, his daytime appetite will improve again. Encourage him to take more solids and milk in the day. Slow down the reduction rate of his feeds for 2–3 nights, until the waking problem has settled again.

What if my baby is due to be fed 4-hourly in the night but wakes after 3½ hours?

If your baby's feed is almost due, it would be better to feed her immediately rather than wait and then feed her.

If she consistently wakes half an hour before the expected feed time, at some point you will have to move her on to the next stage and resettle her without a feed. If she wakes far short of the expected feed time, resettle her without a feed.

What if my baby falls asleep during night feeds. Should I wake him?

If your baby doesn't finish his feed, he may wake, hungry, earlier than expected. If he is becoming increasingly sleepy during his feed, try 'winding' him to see if this rouses him a little. If he has had enough, resettle him. Avoid feeding him before the next feed is due or he may develop a pattern of snacking and napping.

Daytime napping

What if I can't settle my baby with the new technique in the daytime?

At the start of the programme, it is more important to get the timing of the naps right rather than the detail of how she is going to sleep. Once you have gained confidence in settling your baby during the night, you can start to apply the technique during the day.

Sleep-phase problems

What if my child has a late sleep phase but I am reluctant to put him to bed later on a school night?

You will need to correct the problem by waking him up earlier in the morning (see page 79). If that doesn't work, it may be better to wait until his school holiday.

What if I have made bedtime later but my child is still taking a long time to go to sleep?

You probably haven't made bedtime late enough. Delay bedtime 15 minutes at a time until your child is going

to sleep fairly quickly. Make this the starting point of your programme. Recheck your bedtime routine too.

What if my child wakes early in the morning and does not manage to go back to sleep but I need to get ready for work?

This can be a problem when dealing with early rising issues. Wait for a quiet moment. For example, if your child has been crying, wait for a break in the crying and then appear at the bedroom door, announcing that it is time to get up and start the day. If this keeps occurring you need to reassess your programme and decide whether the technique you are using is appropriate to deal with her problem.

What if my child wakes early but has had enough sleep?

There are children who go to sleep alone at bedtime with no problem – often at about 7.00 pm – and sleep all night but wake ready to face the world by 5.30–6.00 am. They are happy children who cope with everyday routines and obviously don't need any more sleep.

You need to teach your child to stay in his bedroom quietly until the rest of the family are ready to get up. Try using a timed lamp (see page 82, Man-made sunrise) – or, if he is older, a digital clock – to indicate when it is all right to engage in quiet play. Try to set clear boundaries on what he is allowed to do, such as staying in bed reading or going downstairs and putting on the TV quietly. If you are allowing your child out of his bedroom, make sure the house is safe to avoid accidents.

In the case of a young baby or toddler, place a couple of soft toys in his cot once he has gone to sleep so that he can play with them when he wakes. You cannot expect a young baby to be silent, but you may be able to steal some quiet moments to gather your thoughts before you start the day!

What if my twins don't sleep at the same time?

If you have twins, you need them to sleep at the same time in order to have a little time off. Establish a set bedtime for them and create a simple routine that will suit both of them simultaneously.

Make sure you stick to it, tucking them both in at the same time, and don't worry about one waking

The timings of your baby's naps can influence her ability and willingness to sleep at night.

the other. As they are used to it, most twins don't seem to get bothered by the other's cries. You may even find that a sleep routine will establish itself more easily with twins, as they encourage and reinforce each other's expectations.

It is tempting to deal straight away with the cries of the noisiest twin, but it is more important to respond to the 'quiet' twin first in order to reinforce appropriate behaviour. You can then deal with the complaining twin.

If the twins have very different sleep patterns, you can try resetting the body clock (see page 79) of the twin whose sleep times are currently causing you the most problems.

What if we are using the 'magic lamp' system but my child can't stay in bed until the lamp is on?

Look at the rewards or incentives you have offered your child – they may not be sufficiently motivating.

Also, you may have set the time too late. You may need to go back a step or two and set the lamp 15 minutes earlier than your child's average waking time. Alternatively, you may be going too fast: try going back to the time that she was achieving and keep it there for a week before moving on again.

If your child continues to get out of bed you may have to apply the door-shutting technique (see page 81).

Rewards

What if my child does not respond to rewards/is not motivated by the sleep fairy?

Try offering a different reward. Send a letter from the sleep fairy as an extra boost. Above all, keep the concept alive. Your child may conveniently forget the reward system if he thinks the task expected of him is too difficult. Re-evaluate the goals you have set him to ensure they are achievable.

You can adapt the rewards and communication with the fairy endlessly. Use your imagination to keep the sleep fairy concept alive and increase your child's motivation (see page 83, Sleep fairy).

5 Identifying the problem

How to use the problem flow charts

Our problem flow charts are designed to help you identify the nature of the problem that you are experiencing. They also direct you to more detailed supporting information elsewhere in the book. This may be in the form of technical descriptions, case studies (Chapter 6, Sleep solutions) or broad background information.

Each flow chart starts with a common problem and goes on to explore the particular aspects of the situation that might apply to a child with this problem. This exploration mirrors the kind of questioning we use at Millpond Children's Sleep Clinic during a consultation, when we are seeking to define the exact nature of the difficulties being experienced by our clients.

In several instances, we have looked at the same problem for a number of age groups because the underlying reasons for that problem, as in the case of night-time feeding, are very different in the early months compared with the later years.

Using the flow charts is simple: first identify the problem that most closely matches your own, then follow the questions and suggestions it contains. As many families know, sleep problems often come in multiples, so you may find that more than one flow chart applies to you.

Any plan you adopt will work best if it is tailored to your particular child's problem, age and circumstances. Your domestic arrangements, your child's personality, your own parenting style and the rate of improvement you are seeking may all play a part in your decision as to what best suits you and your child (see Chapter 4, Tackling sleep problems).

When it comes to implementing a plan, the rule is to keep to it rigidly. Adopting a programme and then diverting from it, or abandoning it, can exacerbate the very problems you hope to solve. However, keeping a sleep diary and reassessing your progress regularly will enable you to make adjustments as necessary.

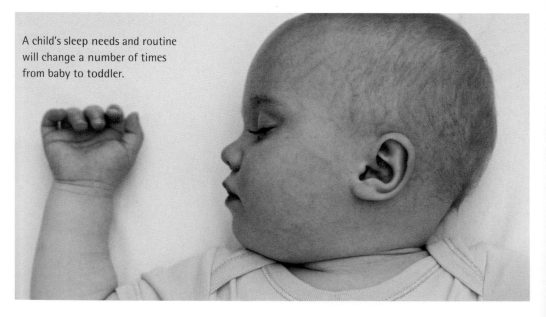

A child's sleep needs and routine will change a number of times from baby to toddler.

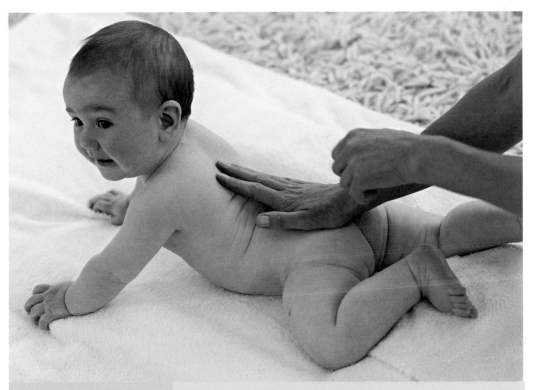

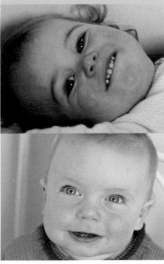

Mini index of flow charts

Flow chart 1 Daytime napping

Daytime sleep can affect night-time sleep profoundly. A child who eats and sleeps well in the day will tend also to sleep regularly and predictably at night, while one who takes short, frequent naps in the daytime may well follow the same pattern at night, waking frequently.

Children who do not nap well also tend to have an impaired appetite, so their entire eating and sleeping schedule is disrupted. Good daytime naps are the foundation of a good night's sleep. Therefore, the solution is not, as many parents believe, to restrict a child's naps in the hope that he will compensate by sleeping longer at night. Instead, it is to focus on the timing and amount of sleep in the day, ensuring it is correct for the child's age.

What kind of napping schedule should your child follow?

Your baby's napping schedule will change with age, but as a general rule the older your child gets the less sleep he will need in the day.

See pages 20–25, Developmental stages and sleep

See page 34, Number and length of naps

Do you have difficulties getting your baby to sleep during the day?

Do you know when your child is tired?
It is important to learn to recognize your baby's sleepy cues in order to avoid over-tiredness.

For signs that your baby is becoming sleepy
see pages 28, Sleep cues

Do you have a structure to your day?
Aim to time your child's naps well. Plan mealtimes so that your child does not fall asleep hungry.

Just as you have a bedtime routine, implement a similar, shorter regime before each nap so that your child is aware of its approach.

See pages 32–35, Naps   See Solution 1

Will your child only settle in the car or pram for daytime naps?

Initially, the timing of naps is more important than where your child is napping. Once your nap schedule is in place and night-time sleep is settled, you can start to teach your child to settle in his cot or bed in the daytime using a sleep-training technique.

See pages 74–81, Sleep-training techniques

See pages 32–35, Naps

See page 53, Inappropriate sleep associations

A pre-nap routine will help your child to establish a regular napping programme.

Does your child have a very late nap and subsequently find it difficult to settle at bedtime?

If you are experiencing settling problems with your child and he is napping late in the afternoon, one of the first things to consider is to bring his nap time forward gradually until bedtime battles cease. Consequently, you may need to make adjustments to your child's mealtimes and other naps to accommodate this change.

See pages 32–33, Spacing: the key to good naps

See page 34, Number and length of naps

See Solution 1

Does your baby take only very short naps?

Cat-naps take the edge off tiredness but if the sleep cycle is not completed your baby will become over-tired and difficult to cope with. This pattern of sporadic sleeping could be repeated during the night.

See page 35, Napping problems

See page 32–33, Spacing: the key to good naps

Flow chart 2 Bedtime battles 0–12 months

Many parents have problems settling their children at this age. They can spend hours in a baby's bedroom attempting to get her to sleep, which not only tests their patience, but results in an over-tired child whose settling problems may be exacerbated by excessive fatigue.

There are a number of possible causes of settling problems: lack of a set bedtime and bedtime routine; over-tiredness; irregular or late daytime naps; and the inability to self-settle.

Does your baby cry heavily around bedtime, making it difficult for you to settle her?

If your baby is crying for long periods in the evening she may have colic, which often gets worse nearer bedtime.

See page 58, Colic and reflux

Does your baby appear to be over-tired at bedtime?
If your child's napping and feeding schedule is irregular or inconsistent this can lead to over-tiredness at bedtime, causing difficulties settling.

See page 34,
Number and
length of naps

See Solution 2

Is your baby over 3 months old and has not yet learned to self-settle?

Have you established a set bedtime and regular routine for your baby?
By 3 months of age your baby has the ability to recognize and respond to sleep cues. By establishing a bedtime and bedtime routine, you can teach your baby healthy sleep patterns.

See pages 30–31,
Creating a sleep
routine

See Solution 1

Do you have to rock, hold or feed your baby to get her to sleep?
Your baby has not learned to self-settle and may have inappropriate sleep associations.

See page 53,
Inappropriate
sleep
associations

See Solution 2

Flow chart 3 Bedtime battles 1–6 years

Settling problems that have not been sorted out in the first year are likely to persist. They may still have the same causes but, as the child develops, additional factors may come into play. These include: over-tiredness after school, anxieties, getting a second wind, or a late sleep phase (an inability to fall asleep until later in the evening).

Do you have to provide certain conditions for your child to go to sleep?

If, for example, your child is in the habit of falling asleep on the sofa, or you sit with him until he goes to sleep at bedtime, he has probably developed inappropriate sleep associations.

See page 53, Inappropriate sleep associations   *See* Solution 3

Does your child refuse to go to bed and keep coming downstairs or calling for you at bedtime?

Do you have a set bedtime with a consistent winding-down routine?
If parents do not set consistent bedtime limits a child may refuse to go to bed or may keep getting out of bed as a consequence. Parents often give in to this behaviour, thereby reinforcing it.

See pages 30–31, Creating a sleep routine   *See page 74–81,* Sleep-training techniques   *See* Solution 5

Does your child have a late nap?
Your child may not be tired enough to go to sleep at an appropriate bedtime.

See pages 32–35, Naps

Is your child anxious or frightened at bedtime?

It is not uncommon for children to experience fears or anxieties at bedtime. The causes of these anxieties will change as your child develops and matures.

See pages 20–25, Developmental stages and sleep

See page 86, What if...?, Bedtime battles

See Solution 4

Flow chart 4 Night waking 0–12 months

Children wake more often at night than we realize, and parents need to teach them the ability to get themselves back to sleep without parental intervention. If a child has no serious physical or emotional cause for sleep disturbances, she needs to be taught to fall asleep alone.

Children can wake at night because they want to feed (see flow charts on pages 102–103 and 104–105). However, this is not always the cause of night waking and you often have to consider other reasons why your baby might be waking. Once you have identified the reason, you can try to eliminate the cause.

Is your baby uncomfortable?

Do you think your child is too hot or too cold?
Your baby's room temperature should be 18 °C (64 °F). Check your baby to see that she is not too hot or too cold. If she throws off her blankets, consider using a baby sleeping bag. This should have a TOG value appropriate for the time of year.

See pages 36–37,
Creating the right environment

Do you think your baby is in pain or unwell?
Your baby may have constipation or colic or, if closer to 6 months old, may be teething. Check her temperature and look for other signs of illness. Call your doctor if you suspect your baby is ill.

See page 47,
Illness

See pages 58–63,
Other problems affecting sleep

Does your baby have nappy rash?
Stinging from nappy rash could be waking your baby when she wets her nappy. Allow time in the day for her to be nappy-free and avoid using baby wipes. Ask your health visitor about a nappy cream.

Do you need to provide certain conditions to enable your child to go back to sleep during the night?

If you need to rock, feed or replace your child's dummy during the night she may have developed an inappropriate sleep association.

See page 53, Inappropriate sleep associations

See page 84, What if...?, General problems

See Solution 7

Are you sure your baby is fully awake?

Many children will drift back to sleep if left undisturbed.

Sometimes you may think your baby is waking when she is just in a phase of light sleep. She may be awake but about to drift back to sleep if left undisturbed.

See pages 18–19, Sleep cycles

Does your baby of over 6 months wake and cry for you during the night?

Has your child only recently started waking regularly in the night?
Your child may have developed separation anxiety. She may be waking because she has become more mobile and her night movements are disturbing her sleep, alternatively she may be teething or unwell.

See pages 20–25, Developmental stages and sleep

See page 47, Illness

See pages 58–63, Other problems affecting sleep

Does your baby have many short daytime naps and also wake frequently at night?
Your baby may be waking at night because she is repeating the same sleep/waking pattern she has developed during the day.

Does your baby need your presence during the night to get back to sleep?
Your baby may have inappropriate sleep associations and only be able to get back to sleep if you are rocking, cuddling or touching her. From 3 months, you may need to consider teaching your baby to self settle, which will help her to resettle herself during the night.

See page 53, Inappropriate sleep associations

See pages 30–31, Creating a sleep routine

See pages 32–33, Spacing: the key to good naps   *See Solution 1*

See Solution 6

Flow chart 5 Night waking 1–6 years

Around 20 per cent of 2 year olds and 5 per cent of 8 year olds wake regularly during the night. Night waking is essentially caused by a child's inability to self-settle and is especially frustrating when you know that your child is not waking for a feed, particularly if he has previously been sleeping well but has now started to wake.

Certain events can trigger night waking, such as illness, a holiday, moving house or moving from a cot into a bed.

If night wakings are inadvertently rewarded with contact from parents they can become habitual. Nipping the problem in the bud is important because the more quickly you deal with it, the easier it will be.

Do you have to provide certain conditions in the night for your child to go back to sleep?

If your child needs certain conditions to go back to sleep in the night, for example, you lay or sit with him, and you also provide the same things at bedtime, your child has acquired inappropriate sleep associations. You need to teach him to self-settle.

See page 53, Inappropriate sleep associations

See pages 74–81, Sleep-training techniques

See Solutions 8 *and* 9

Avoid lying down with your child as a means to sleep.

A move from a cot to a bed can result in a bout of night waking.

Does your child keep calling out for you or coming to find you in the night?

Your child may be dependent on seeing you during the night to be able to get back to sleep and, if he is in a bed, will physically seek you out.

See pages 74–81, Sleep-training techniques

See Solution 12

Have you recently transferred your child from a cot to a bed?
Moving from cot to bed can provide your child with a new-found freedom. Until your child has understood new night-time rules the problem may persist.

See pages 74–81, Sleep-training techniques   *See* Solution 10

Does your child wake and appear frightened or anxious?
Your child could be experiencing a night terror, a nightmare or fear of the dark.

See page 37, Fear of the dark   *See pages 56–57,* Nightmares and night terrors

Does your older child wake because he has wet the bed?

See pages 62–63, Bed-wetting

Flow chart 6 Night feeding 0–6 months

With very rare exceptions, young babies of this age will wake up during the night to feed. It is inevitably tiring for parents, but there are ways of coping with and managing the situation.

Newborn babies have tiny stomachs the size of a fist and therefore need to feed frequently. For at least the first 6 weeks, sleeping and eating go hand in hand, and babies will often fall asleep straight after a feed or while feeding.

If you are breast-feeding, it is undesirable to try to drop night feeds too early because these feeds ensure that your hormone levels remain constant, thus helping to maintain a good milk supply. As your baby's sleep patterns settle and she can sleep for longer stretches at a time, night feeds will become less frequent. After this, a pattern begins to emerge and you can start to manage night feeds so that you have more opportunity to sleep yourself.

Does your baby sleep for most of the day, but stay awake feeding at night?

Your baby will sleep in stretches of 2–3 hours at a time, after which she will wake up, feed and fall back to sleep. These periods are spread throughout the day and night. It can take 6–10 weeks for her to develop a good 24-hour schedule, with the longest period of sleep occurring at night. It is rare for a baby under 6 weeks old to sleep more than 6 hours at a stretch at night.

See pages 28–29, Get into a rhythm: the first 3 months

See pages 74–81, Sleep-training techniques

Has your baby suddenly started to wake more at night for feeds?

Your baby may be having a growth spurt, which means she needs to feed more frequently in the day to sustain her at night. Growth spurts seem to occur at around 1–3 weeks, 6–8 weeks, 3 months and 6 months of age.

See pages 20–25, Developmental stages and sleep

See pages 74–75, Night-feed weaning

A baby will sleep for longer at night once regular daytime feeds are established.

Does your 4–6-month-old baby wake frequently for night feeds?

Have you started a bedtime routine yet?
From 3 months onwards, you can start a bedtime routine. If your baby can settle herself at bedtime, she may start to do so when she wakes in the night.

By 3–4 months most babies will have adopted regular patterns of waking and sleeping. Sleep should improve at this age because it will be regulated by the baby's maturing body clock. If you are still on a newborn feeding schedule at this age, it should be possible to space your baby's feeds so that you all get a better night's sleep. As your baby approaches 6 months there is no need for her to have night feeds. You may have a baby who has learned to associate sucking with sleeping.

See pages 74–75,
Night-feed weaning

See pages 18–19,
Sleep cycles

See page 53,
Inappropriate sleep associations

See Solution 13

See pages 30–31,
Creating a sleep routine

Flow chart 7 Night feeding from 6 months

From 6 months almost all babies should be ready to stop night feeds. Waking for milk may be caused by three factors: your baby has learned to be hungry; he associates feeding with going to sleep in the evening and getting back to sleep in the night; and he enjoys the reward of being close to you at this time.

Frequent night feeding disrupts a baby's ability to learn to sleep through the night. The extra fluid will stimulate your child's digestive system when it should be shutting down. It also disrupts the sleep–wake cycle, so a child may get stuck on an infant schedule and view the sleep between night feeds as naps.

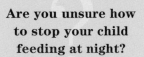

Are you unsure how to stop your child feeding at night?

Does your child feed hungrily during the night?
As a general rule, if a child over 6 months old wakes more than twice a night and drinks large amounts (8 fl oz/240 ml or more of formula, or breast-feeding more than once or twice a night for more than 5–10 minutes), he may have a night-feeding problem. Your aim is gradually to decrease the amount of milk offered until night feeds are eliminated.

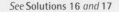

See pages 74–75,
Night-feed weaning

See Solutions 16 *and* 17

Does your child have short frequent feeds in the night after which he generally settles immediately?
If your child settles on the breast or bottle at bedtime, falls asleep normally after being fed during the night and only takes small amounts of milk, he may have developed inappropriate sleep associations. You need gradually to wean him off night feeds and teach him to self-settle.

See page 53,
Inappropriate sleep associations

See pages 74–75,
Night-feed weaning

See Solutions 14 *and* 15

Your child should no longer need to rely on a night-time feed from the age of 6 months.

Are you concerned how to settle your baby at night without feeding him?

Once you have weaned your baby off night feeds it is time to teach him to self-settle. To guarantee a good night's sleep, you will need to ensure your baby can self-settle at bedtime as well as during the night. It is important to choose a technique that will suit you as a family.

See page 53, Inappropriate sleep associations

See pages 74–81, Sleep-training techniques

See Solutions 14, 15, 16 and 17

Flow chart 8 Early rising

Early morning waking is one of the most exhausting problems for parents and is also often one of the most difficult to solve, especially if there are no other sleep-related issues. This can be caused by: a hungry child who wakes early for a feed and then refuses to go back to sleep; excessive daytime naps; an exceptionally early bedtime; or receiving rewards such as watching the television or getting into the parents' bed for waking early. It may also be due to environmental factors. However, some children are natural larks, or simply need less sleep.

Is your child sensitive to environmental factors?

Check whether your child's room is too light, too warm or too cold. Is there any noise that might be disturbing her?

See pages 36–37, Creating the right environment

Is your child having too much daytime sleep?

Is your baby ready to nap within an hour of getting up?
Needing to sleep so soon after getting up in the morning would suggest that this nap is an extension of her night-time sleep. You will need gradually to move this nap later each morning, aiming for it to take place between 2–3 hours after waking.

Does your child fall asleep in the early evening, sleep through the night but wake very early in the morning?

If your baby is sleeping too much during the day, this may be a cause of early waking, as she may take this sleep from her night quota.

As your child's natural night-time sleep period is taken too early within the 24-hour day you will need gradually to delay bedtime until the sleep period has shifted to an appropriate time.

See pages 32–33, Spacing: the key to good naps

See pages 32–35, Naps, and pages 16–17, What is normal sleep?

See pages 20–25, Developmental stages and sleep

See pages 16–17, What is normal sleep?

See page 79, Early sleep phase – method

Does your baby wake for an early morning feed?

Is she over 6 months old and waking for a morning feed around 5.00 am and not going back to sleep?
Your baby has learned to be hungry at this time. If your baby is well and thriving, you can begin to wean her off this feed gently or to shift it later gradually, so that she doesn't expect a feed this early in the morning. She will soon learn to have her milk quota during the day.

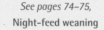

See pages 74–75,
Night-feed weaning

See Solution 18

Are you inadvertently encouraging early rising by rewarding your child's behaviour?

If your child has the incentive to wake early, that is, by coming into your bed for an early cuddle, she has learned to wake at this hour. To stop this habit you need to stop the incentive and encourage your child to stay in her bed.

See pages 74–81,
Sleep-training techniques

See pages 82–83,
Positive reinforcement – rewards

See Solution 18

Does your child seem to need less sleep than other children?

Some children really do need less sleep. They wake early but appear rested and happy, and cope well with daily routines. In fact, most children have had the majority of their sleep by 5.00 am and the drive to return to sleep at this time is greatly reduced. Some children will wake to start the day.

See pages 16–17,
What is normal sleep?

See pages 88–89,
What if...?,
Sleep-phase problems

Flow chart 9 Settling late/ late bedtime

If a child is physically unable to fall asleep until after the desired bedtime, it may result in bedtime battles. Once asleep he sleeps well and, if left, would naturally wake late in the morning. However, he is often tired in the day because he has to be woken to start daily routines. His sleep period has shifted to later in the evening, creating what is known as a 'late sleep phase'. It can affect children of all ages. The problem often arises when sleeping times are not consistently maintained, common reasons for disturbances are: holidays, temporary fears or anxieties, illness or an irregular schedule.

Does your child's natural sleep period happen too late in the day?

Do you have problems waking your child in the morning?
It is likely that your child is not getting enough sleep for his age. You will need to keep a sleep diary for 1 week to enable you to work out what time he is naturally falling asleep. You will need gradually to shift his body clock so that he falls asleep at a more appropriate time, thereby waking naturally in the morning.

See pages 72–73,
Keeping a sleep diary

See pages 16–17,
What is normal sleep?

See pages 79–81,
Late sleep phase – method

See Solution 19

Do you struggle to get your child to bed at 'bedtime'?
Your expectations for your child's bedtime may be earlier than the time your child is naturally ready to sleep, resulting in bedtime battles. You will need to keep a sleep diary for 1 week to enable you to work out what time your child is naturally falling asleep. Once you have established this, you can then gradually shift his sleep phase earlier, using the late sleep phase programme, until you have reached the desired sleeping times.

See pages 72–73, Keeping a sleep diary

See pages 79–81,
Late sleep phase – method

See Solution 19

Flow chart 10 Nightmares and night terrors

More than 30 per cent of pre-school children suffer from various forms of sleep disruptions. Almost all have nightmares, which are frightening dreams that require reassurance from their parents. A smaller proportion suffers from night terrors, sleep-walking and sleep-talking, although most children outgrow these by the age of 6 years.

Parents can find it most distressing to see their child upset by a nightmare or seemingly terrified while experiencing a night terror, but these are rarely harmful. Nightmares and the much less common night terrors are actually quite different phenomena (see page 57).

Does your child wake in the first third of the night, screaming?

Does your child appear frightened, scream loudly and become hot and sweaty? Your child may have a 'glassy look', with eyes wide open, apparently not knowing you are there. She will not respond to you but, after a few minutes, she will return to sleep and will not remember the episode in the morning. Your child has probably had a night terror.

See pages 54–57, Sleep disturbances

See Solution 20

Does your child wake, afraid and crying, in the early hours of the morning?

Your child has most probably had a nightmare. Children remember nightmares and, if old enough, can describe them to you. They become fully alert when awake and recognize you. They need reassurance to get back to sleep, which can take some time.

See page 56–57, Nightmares and night terrors

6

Sleep solutions

How to use the solutions

The accounts in this section are all genuine cases that we have dealt with at Millpond Children's Sleep Clinic. They show how families whose children have been experiencing sleep problems have worked to overcome those problems. They represent the range of techniques that can be used to tackle the problems.

You will find that the flow charts in Chapter 5 (Identifying the problem), which address specific problems, and the techniques outlined in Chapter 4 will often direct you to these numbered solutions. In this way you can see how parents have successfully treated real-life sleep problems by following the clearly defined techniques outlined in previous sections of this book. One such solution might work to solve your child's sleep problem.

Each solution is set out in the same way. Firstly there is a detailed description of the problem, explaining how it manifested itself in everyday life and its impact on the child and the family. Next there is a diagnosis that analyses the key problem. This leads on to the plan. This takes into account the family circumstances and outlines the best strategy for dealing with the key problem in such a situation.

This is followed by the result: a brief examination of what happened when the plan was implemented. In this way, you are taken from the diagnosis to the resolution of the child's sleep problem.

Finally, the individual steps of the plan are set out on the right-hand page giving you practical guidance on how to apply this problem at home. Your situation is unlikely to match exactly the case and family circumstances outlined, but you will be able to draw lessons – and encouragement – from what you read. Find the problem that most closely matches yours and then apply the solution.

You should begin to see how the disciplined application of techniques and principles outlined earlier in the book can be applied to a whole range of problems in a wide variety of circumstances. In this sense, it is the combination of clearly defined pro-grammes and the flexibility of their application that can be seen to work in practice. You will find that consistency and commitment will bring their reward.

If you are starting to read this book by referring to the solutions described here, you will find pointers to the earlier sections of the book that explain the techniques or sleep programmes in more detail. Carefully applied, they should bring you the same success – and welcome rest.

To tackle your child's sleep problem you need to be fully committed to stick to a programme.

Mini index of case studies

Solution 1 **Daytime napping**

Try this gradual-retreat plan if, like Ruby, your young baby has very disruptive and irregular sleep routines.

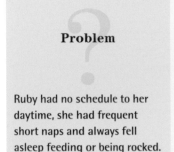

Problem

Ruby had no schedule to her daytime, she had frequent short naps and always fell asleep feeding or being rocked.

Ruby was 12 weeks old with no siblings. She slept in a cot in her parents' room and, most of the time, in their bed.

She had suffered from colic since birth, which meant her parents found it difficult to establish a routine. In the evening, she was breast-fed to sleep and placed in her car seat in the sitting room. Her parents found this suited them better as Ruby fed on and off most of the evening. She finally settled in her cot when her parents went to bed at 11.00 pm. Ruby woke two to four times every night and was breast-fed back to sleep each time. She woke to start the day at 9.00 am.

Diagnosis

Ruby had no set bedtime or bedtime routine. She had learned to go to sleep on the breast and associated this with sleep. As Ruby was feeding frequently at night, she viewed sleeping at night-time as naps between feeds and was not having long periods of sleep. Her night-time sleep was mirrored in her daytime pattern.

Plan

Ruby's parents needed to decide on a suitable bedtime for her, and to arrive at that time gradually. They settled on 7.30 pm and established a relaxing, bedtime routine making sure Ruby's pre-bed feed was given before starting the process.

Ruby had been settling at 11.00 pm, so bedtime was brought forward by 30 minutes for the first 3 nights and she was to be woken 30 minutes earlier in the morning. This process was repeated every 3 days until Ruby was going to bed at 7.30 pm and starting the day at 6.30/7.00 am.

Ruby's parents used a gradual-retreat programme to teach Ruby to self-settle, starting with rocking her to sleep at bedtime and when she woke during the night if not a feed time. Ruby's night feeds were scheduled: she was offered her last daytime feed before starting the bedtime routine. During the night she was fed no more than 3 hourly.

Results

Ruby cried for nearly an hour on the first night of the programme, with her parents rocking her to sleep. She woke almost on the hour throughout the night but her parents were determined to stick to the plan and feed her only as scheduled. Daytime was equally stressful and Ruby's mother had difficulty keeping her awake, feeding and sleeping at the scheduled times. As the week progressed, settling at bedtime improved. Ruby protested less and was asleep within 20 minutes.

By the start of the second week Ruby was being settled in her cot. Initially she found this difficult and cried for long periods. By the end of this week she had accepted settling in her cot and was usually managing to go 3 hours between night feeds. During the day, Ruby was taken out in her pushchair for her midday nap, where she usually slept for 2 hours. Her mother continued to settle her in her cot for her other naps.

By the end of week 3, bedtime had been brought forward to 7.30 pm. Ruby was self-settling with her parents sitting away from the cot. She was waking to start the day between 6.00 am and 6.30 am. She had dropped one of her night feeds completely and was generally waking around 4.00 am for a feed and settling well after the feed. Most of her daytime naps were now taken in the cot. Ruby's daytime feeds were taken 4 hourly after her naps.

Steps

Teach your baby to disassociate her last feed with bedtime by feeding her before starting her bedtime routine.

Step 1 Have a consistent time for bed. If your child currently goes to bed later than you wish, bring her bedtime forward by 30 minutes every fourth night. If your child is also starting her day late, you will need to wake her 30 minutes earlier every fourth day until you reach your desired wake-up time.

Step 2 Offer the last daytime feed before you start the bedtime routine, not letting your baby fall asleep, so she learns to disassociate feeding with sleep. Establish a relaxing, consistent bedtime routine focused around her bedroom and lasting no longer than 45 minutes (see page 30, Creating a sleep routine).

Step 3 Choose a sleep-training technique to teach your child to self-settle that will suit both you and your baby (see page 74, Sleep-training techniques).

Step 4 If your baby is a frequent night-time feeder you will need to begin to 'space' the feeds (see page 75, Schedule for reducing or spacing feeds).

Step 5 To establish good daytime routines, avoid allowing your baby to take frequent 'cat-naps', but space the time between naps so that the nap becomes longer but is the appropriate amount of time for your child's age (see page 32, Naps).

Suggested daytime routine for a baby of 3–6 months	
Time	Activity
6.30–7.00 am	Wake-up time
7.00 am	Wake-up feed
8.30 am	Nap (approx 45–60 minutes)
11.00 am	Feed (after nap)
12.00 pm	Nap (approx 90–120 minutes)
3.00 pm	Feed
4.00 pm	Nap (approx 45–60 minutes)
6.30 pm	Feed

Solution 2 Bedtime battles 0–12 months

Try this plan if, like Billy, your baby has erratic, inconsistent bedtimes, irregular naps and no pattern to his night-time sleep.

? Problem

Billy was 7 months old and an only child. From birth he would not go to sleep in his cot, but would only settle if breast-fed to sleep or held in his mother's arms.

Quote from mother 'Billy's father and I spend very little time together. He is keen to let Billy cry, but I am not sure, as there must be another way.'

Billy's daytime routines were erratic, with no set naps or mealtimes. His daytime naps totalled about 1 hour, consisting of two 30-minute sessions - considerably less than the 3–3½ hours appropriate for his age.

On a typical night he was fed at around 6.00 pm, given a quick bath at 6.30 pm, when he was usually getting tired, and then breast-fed for 10-30 minutes until asleep. He was then lifted into his cot very carefully to prevent him waking.

However, Billy would usually rouse soon after, thrashing his arms around and crying. His mother would pick him up and put him back on the breast. Half an hour later he would wake up again and his mother would then take him into the parents' room, where she would lie down and feed him while watching television. By about 10.00 pm he would have finally fallen asleep and could be carried back to his own room and placed in his cot.

This pattern continued throughout the night, every night, with Billy waking four to five times, being breast-fed in his parents bed until asleep and then eventually placed back in his own cot. As a consequence, Billy's day started anywhere between 7.00 am and 9.00 am.

Diagnosis

Billy had no structure or routine by day or night: he had learned to fight sleep and was chronically sleep-deprived. He had no set bedtime or regular bedtime routine. He associated breast-feeding and close contact with his mother with sleep. He would finally fall asleep late, out of sheer exhaustion. The knock-on effect was that his day often started late, subsequently offsetting his daytime feed/sleep patterns. Billy was unable to settle by himself at night and so was unable to take himself back to sleep without breast-feeding again.

Plan

To regulate Billy's body clock, it was essential to structure his day. His parents established a good

bedtime routine with a regular time for bed. They used the controlled-crying method to teach Billy to settle himself, not only at bedtime, but also when he woke during the night. Finally, to wean Billy off night feeds, his parents agreed to just one feed, which was not to be before midnight. In the morning they woke Billy at 7.00 am if he was not awake already. Three daytime naps were planned and three mealtimes set.

Results

On the first night of the programme, Billy cried for 2 hours at bedtime, but was asleep by 10.30 pm and slept through to 7.00 am. Subsequently, he settled more quickly at bedtime but still took 45 minutes to go to sleep. He woke once in the night at around

4.30 am for a 10-minute feed and then settled well into his cot until morning. He still had problems with daytime naps.

During the second week bedtime was brought forward to 7.30 pm as Billy was very over-tired and failed to settle quickly. His daytime naps proved more difficult to establish, so his parents concentrated on the timing of the naps rather than how or where Billy

was settling, and planned to apply controlled crying once the naps had been established. His night-time feed was shifted to after 4.00 am.

After 2 weeks, Billy was settling at 7.30 pm. He was sleeping through to 5.00 am and, once fed, settled quickly and slept to 7.00 am. He was taking solids at regular times and had two good naps in his cot – one in the morning and one at lunchtime.

Steps

Establishing a regular bedtime routine early on is key to a good sleep programme.

Step 1 If your baby settles late, set a bedtime that is more in tune with his 'sleepy' time. As he learns to settle easily, gradually bring the bedtime forward. Offer a pre-bed feed 15–30 minutes prior to starting the bedtime routine, but do not let him fall asleep during this feed (see page 30, Creating a sleep routine).

Step 2 If your baby is still over-tired at bedtime, bring his bedtime forward by 15 minutes every 2–3 days until you reach the desired time.

Step 3 If your baby is over 6 months old and you would like to stop night feeds, you can either increase the time between feeds thus spacing them and finally moving them through to waking up time, or you can reduce the amount of milk for each feed,

for example, by 1 minute a night if breast-feeding or 1 fl oz (30 ml) a night if bottle feeding (see page 74, Night-feed weaning).

Step 4 If your baby is reluctant to nap during the day, focus on the timing of naps rather than how he gets to sleep. By taking him for a walk in the pushchair or a drive in the car you can regulate the timing. Once naps are established, you can apply a sleep-training technique (see page 74). Start working on one nap at a time. If your baby has not settled within 45 minutes – abandon this nap and try again the next nap time.

Suggested daytime routine for a baby of 6–12 months	
Time	Activity
7.00 am	Morning feed
8.00 am	Breakfast
9.00 am	Nap
10.00 am	Feed
12.00 pm	Lunch
1.00 pm	Nap
3.00 pm	Feed
4.00 pm	Short nap
5.00 pm	Tea
6.30 pm	Pre-bed feed
7.00 pm	Bed

Solution 3 Bedtime battles 1–6 years

Try this plan if, like Hannah, your child has inappropriate sleep associations.

Problem

Hannah was 2½ years old and lived with her mother, a single parent. She had always fallen asleep downstairs and been carried to bed. But, with age, she became more reluctant to settle.

As a baby Hannah would fall asleep feeding from a bottle on her mother's lap; later it was with a bottle on the sofa, after which she was carried to bed. Once asleep she slept all night. At 2½ years, however, Hannah had started running around, not wanting to settle down on the sofa. Her bedtime was getting later and later.

Hannah's mother wanted her to go to sleep at 8.00 pm. Hannah was tired during the day and her mother said she had dark circles under her eyes. She was also throwing more tantrums and her appetite had deteriorated.

Quote from mother *'I want to take some control over the situation as I feel Hannah is dictating what happens in the evening. Hannah needs more sleep and I am worried that it is having a knock-on effect on her daytime behaviour.'*

Diagnosis

On the sofa, Hannah could see her toys and the television was on, so she was finding it hard to go to sleep. She had learned to fall asleep on the sofa and therefore associated this with bedtime. This meant that she could not fall asleep by herself in bed. As there were very few boundaries at bedtime Hannah didn't quite know what was required of her.

Plan

The plan was to establish a fixed bedtime with a winding-down routine. Hannah's mother applied a gradual-retreat programme to teach her how to fall asleep in her own bed at 8.00 pm. This was supported by rewards from the sleep fairy for going to sleep nicely at bedtime.

Results

Progress was excellent. Hannah's mother described the first night as 'amazing': Hannah called out to her

mother a few times but was asleep after 15 minutes. She loved the idea of the sleep fairy, responded well to the new routine and was asleep in her bed by 8.15 pm. She was given her reward in the morning. Night 2 was better and she went to sleep after calling out only once.

On night 3 Hannah got up once to check that her mother was there but was led back to bed and after a couple of calls, to which her mother did not respond, was asleep. Thereafter, Hannah's progress was fairly typical – a good night followed by a not so good night.

After week 2 Hannah lost interest in the sleep fairy and was no longer checking her reward pot. She was also no longer having as many tantrums and her appetite was better.

By the end of week 3, her mother had moved the chair into her own room and Hannah was falling asleep in her own bed. She called out on the odd occasion but was reassured by a quick call of 'Go to sleep Hannah'.

Steps

7.00 pm; straight to his bedroom for bedtime stories; and a goodnight kiss at 7.45 pm. Resist any protests calmly but firmly. Keep bedtime relaxing and calm (see page 30, Creating a sleep routine).

Step 1 If your child is used to falling asleep while feeding, or settles only on the sofa, you need to establish a bedtime routine. For example: pre-bed milk downstairs at 6.45 pm; bath at

Step 2 Apply a gradual-retreat programme (see page 76). Sit with your child until he is asleep. Initially you may need to be close to his bedside, but there should be minimal interaction. Meet any

responses from your child with: 'Go to sleep, Mummy will stay here until you are asleep'. Once your child is asleep, it is important to wait an extra 10 minutes before leaving the room to ensure he is in a deep sleep.

It your child gets out of bed to check your position, do not pick him up but lead him back to his bed, getting him to climb in by himself. Then resume your position on the chair. If he continues to get up to check, use the door-shutting technique (see page 81).

Step 3 Your child may take a while to go to sleep in the first few days as he adjusts to the change in routine. Make sure he fully understands the reward system and use stars or small rewards from the sleep fairy to encourage him (see page 82, Positive reinforcement – rewards).

Step 4 If your child is over 2 years of age, daytime naps should be no longer than 60 to 75 minutes and always avoided after 3.00 pm.

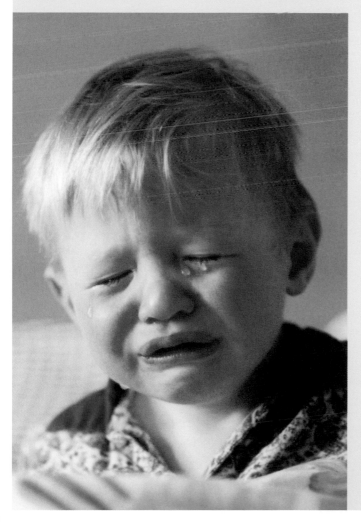

A gradual-retreat programme is less stressful for the child, who is always aware of his parent's presence.

Solution 4 **Bedtime battles 1–6 years**

Try this plan if, like Robert, your child is anxious and unable to get to sleep at bedtime.

Problem

Robert was 6 years old, with a younger sister, and had never slept well. His parents had tried controlled crying but it hadn't worked. They had consulted a doctor and a child psychologist but things were getting worse.

Robert was not an anxious child during the daytime, but would get anxious as bedtime approached. He had been put in a room with his sister in the hope that his anxiety would diminish.

On a typical evening Robert would be getting ready for bed at 7.00–7.15 pm. He would have a bath, brush his teeth, listen to a story and lie in his room, awake. His mother would stay with him for 5 minutes then say goodnight and carry out some quiet activities nearby.

Robert would keep getting out of bed, saying 'I can't get to sleep', and becoming more anxious and distressed. In the end his mother would have to sit outside the room until he was asleep, which could take 1–2 hours.

This had gone on for many years. Robert's mother was desperate for help, as nothing seemed to work.

Diagnosis

Robert's difficulties settling at bedtime had become habitual. What might have started as a common settling problem as a young baby had persisted and developed into a chronic habit: Robert had never truly learned to go to sleep on his own. With age, his anxieties had increased. He was now aware of being awake for long periods and was unable to drop off without a parent being present to give him the necessary safety and security. Robert needed to learn to fall asleep by himself.

Plan

Robert's parents were advised to adjust his bedtime routine and to use a gradual-retreat programme in conjunction with a reward system. This would give Robert more confidence in his ability to go to sleep alone, with positive reinforcement providing him with an incentive. As Robert's ability to sleep was dependent on his mother being upstairs at bedtime, it was decided that step one of the programme should start from the landing outside his bedroom door. The distance was increased gradually by moving down one stair at a time until Robert's mother was finally downstairs when he went to sleep. As Robert was naturally falling asleep late, his new bedtime was set to coincided with this time. It was gradually brought forward as he learned to fall asleep within 15–20 minutes, until a more appropriate bedtime for his age was reached.

Results

Robert made good initial progress, was asleep within 15 minutes of saying 'goodnight' and not coming out to check if his mother was there. He liked the reward system and was already much more positive about bedtime and life in general.

His mother continued to move down the stairs and adjusted Robert's routine, gradually bringing bedtime forward. By night 7, he was in bed by 8.40 pm and asleep by 8.55 pm. He was not checking for his mother at all and she had made it halfway down the stairs.

After 3 weeks he had made further progress and was falling asleep at 8.30 pm and his bedtime anxieties had disappeared entirely.

Steps

Step 1 Begin by keeping a sleep diary for a week in order to establish when your child naturally falls asleep (see page 72, Keeping a sleep diary). If, for example, he usually falls asleep at 9.30 pm, then add 15 minutes to this time, giving 9.45 pm. Your initial aim is to have your child asleep by this time.

Always allow 30–45 minutes for your bedtime routine and work out your timings based on this. For example, start the bedtime routine at 9.00 pm and say goodnight at 9.30 pm; your child should then be asleep by 9.45 pm. Keep the bedtime routine calm and focused (see page 30, Creating a sleep routine). Don't mention bedtime during the evening, but encourage your child to play quietly, for example by colouring or reading.

Once your child has achieved this for at least 3 nights you can start to move your routine forward by 15 minutes. For example, start at 8.45 pm, say goodnight at 9.15 pm and expect your child to be asleep by 9.30 pm. Continue this process every 4 to 7 nights, until your child is falling asleep at the desired time. If he does not fall asleep within

A child can be fresh and confident by day and yet express genuine anxieties come night-time.

15–20 minutes, continue with the same timing for an extra 3 nights. If this still does not work, move the time back by 15 minutes for 3 nights. Do not move it forward again until your child falls asleep within the allotted time period (see page 79, Late sleep phase – method) To see how much sleep is appropriate for the age of your child, check the sleep needs chart on page 17.

Step 2 Apply a gradual-retreat programme (see page 76 for details). This can be carried out in conjunction with the above steps for bedtime changes. Your starting position will depend on the age of your child and the difficulties you are experiencing at bedtime.

Solution 5 Bedtime battles 1–6 years

Try this plan if, like Jake, your child refuses to go to bed and keeps coming downstairs or calling for you at bedtime.

Problem

Jake was 3½ years old, attended nursery five mornings a week and no longer had a nap in the day. He and his older brother had their own bedrooms.

Quote from parent 'We feel so helpless as parents. We just don't know how to keep Jake in his bed and we know 9.00 pm is too late for a child of his age to go to sleep.'

Jake's sleep problems started when the family moved to a new house and Jake had his own room for the first time. After the excitement wore off and the reality of sleeping in his own room struck him, he started resisting bedtime. Even with the promise of a reward in the morning, Jake found it difficult to stay in bed.

Although his parents began to get him ready for bed at 6.00 pm, Jake was never asleep before 9.00 pm. Once asleep he would sleep through to the morning and his mother had to wake him at 7.30 am. At weekends he would naturally sleep until 8.45 am.

The bedtime routine involved both boys. They had a bath together for 20 minutes or so, and would then have a little run around. After getting them into their nightclothes the mother read two stories in the brother's room before taking Jake to his room. Their father often came home from work towards the end of this bedtime routine and would talk and share in their fun and games.

Jake's parents were concerned that Jake was not getting enough sleep: he always fell asleep in the car, even on short journeys. They also felt that he threw too many tantrums and became upset too easily.

Diagnosis

Jake's settling problem had been provoked by anxieties over having a room of his own, and was compounded by the inappropriately stimulating bedtime routine.

He was well on the way to developing a late sleep phase. By the time he tried to go to sleep he had got a second wind and was unable to go to sleep until he had a chance to get tired again, which was an hour or so later. His continual coming downstairs and calling out was a result of being unable to get to sleep in this aroused state.

Plan

Jake needed to learn to fall asleep within the normal range of 15–20 minutes once he had said goodnight

to his parents, to sleep through to the morning, and to wake naturally 11½ or 12 hours later.

The parents devised an appropriate bedtime routine, with an emphasis on a proper, relaxing wind-down period leading up to bed. Any wild or rough-and-tumble play took place before supper, and suppertime marked a clear division between daytime activities and bedtime. After supper the boys had a special quiet time with their mother, reading or drawing.

A reward system was set up to encourage Jake to settle to sleep at bedtime without getting up or calling out. His parents were keen to try the sleep fairy, but only on the understanding there were no battles at bedtime! His parents job was to 'hook' Jake on to the idea of the fairy.

Results

Jake's parents very successfully implemented a bedtime routine and both boys seemed a lot calmer at bedtime as a result. His mother felt the reward system had helped with this. Jake was no longer coming downstairs or calling out. In the first 2 days it took him longer than 20 minutes to go to sleep: his parents often heard him talking or singing to himself. Even so, by the end of the first week, the latest he had fallen asleep was 8.15 pm and in the following weeks he was always asleep by 8.00 pm, a whole hour earlier than before the programme.

Steps

If your child refuses to stay in bed at bedtime, try implementing the door-shutting technique (see page 81).

Step 1 If you have a child who expects a lively evening and takes time to wind down, start his bedtime routine about 45 minutes before the time you want him to be asleep. Keep bathtime brief – it may need supervision if it is shared by siblings. Shortening the time in the bath even further and limiting the amount of bath toys will help to get your child in the right frame of mind. If you have two or more children, you may want to consider separate bath times. Explain the importance of a quiet bedtime routine to your partner: his/her involvement is important but it must be a calm procedure (see page 30, Creating a sleep routine).

After a bath, get your children straight into their own bedrooms. The oldest can put on his nightclothes and read a book while waiting for you or your partner to come and read a story. You can set up a reward system to encourage this behaviour.

Step 2 About 45 minutes after starting the routine, say goodnight. Offer an appropriate reward from the sleep fairy for not calling out or getting out of bed after bedtime.

Step 3 If it takes a little while for your child's body clock to reset itself and for him to relearn the ability to settle to sleep quickly, do not despair. Stick faithfully to the new routine and be consistent and clear about the bedtime boundaries. Work as a team with your partner to maintain consistency and – with a little more time – you will achieve your goal. You can expect a marked change in your child's expectations and consequent behaviour within 2–3 weeks.

Solution 6 Night waking 0–12 months

Try this controlled-crying plan if, like Sam, your child is under 1 year old, settles well at bedtime, but wakes in the night and refuses to go back to sleep.

? Problem

Sam was 11 months old. He slept in a cot in his own room, but cried for long periods at night. His mother slept in the spare room during the week and his father attended to him when he woke. They swapped duties at weekends.

Quote from mother 'Sleep deprivation makes us both short tempered. We sleep in separate rooms and see little of each other.'

Sam's sleep had always been erratic. He settled alone perfectly well at bedtime, but woke, crying, once or twice each night, often for a couple of hours at a time. During the day he napped for 2 hours around lunchtime.

At night-time, Sam had a bath at 6.00 pm, followed by a bottle of formula milk at 6.30 pm and bed at 7.00 pm. Although seemingly very awake, he would go to sleep almost immediately in his own bed, alone, and never had a problem with bedtime.

However, he usually woke at around 3 am. His parent would wait 10–15 minutes before going in, keeping the light very low, and change his nappy if dirty. Otherwise, he or she would put a hand on his chest and 'shh' him for a minute or two and then leave, at which point Sam would become very angry. This would be repeated every 10–15 minutes for up to 2–3 hours in the night. His parents rarely picked him up.

The situation caused a great deal of strain for Sam's parents. His mother had been under pressure at work and both parents were worried. They had tried controlled crying – extending the time between visits – but with no success.

Diagnosis

Sam had a night-waking problem. He settled well at bedtime but was unable to take himself back to sleep in the night. His parents' constant visits to his room during waking episodes were preventing Sam from learning to self-settle. He eventually fell asleep through exhaustion.

Plan

The objective was to reduce Sam's level of contact with his parents during the night so that he could learn to go back to sleep by himself. His parents applied the controlled-crying technique together with a consistent bedtime routine that was to take no longer than 30 minutes. For a 7.00 pm bedtime, they offered a bottle

feed at 6.00–6.15 pm, followed by a bath. They got Sam into nightclothes by 6.30 pm, then into bed with a story. After a goodnight kiss, his parent left the room.

Whenever Sam woke during the night, his parents applied controlled crying. They were advised not to touch him or go too close to his cot when going into his room – something they found difficult because they had always touched him.

Results

On the first night of the programme, Sam settled well into the new bedtime routine. He woke once during the night and his parents carried out controlled crying for 1½ hours before he went back to sleep. His mother found the crying very distressing. Soon after starting the programme, Sam caught a cold so the programme was disrupted. The parents were able to continue with the bedtime routine but would not let Sam cry in the night as he had a high temperature. During this period they cuddled him back to sleep.

By day 11 Sam was much better and the family were able to resume the programme. On day 13, his parents reported that, for the previous 2 nights, Sam had slept through the night to 5.15 am. At this point they attempted to get him back to sleep using controlled crying. This was abandoned after 2 hours of crying, when they decided to get on and start the day.

Sam's mother was finding the early morning crying difficult to cope with. To relieve some pressure the parents were advised to get up and start the day if Sam was waking after 5.00 am. If the early waking persisted after 2–3 days, they should try not to go in to Sam's room until 6.00 am, but leave him to cry until this time. By day 17, Sam had slept to 6.00 am on four occasions, and his parents were very happy with his progress. Sam is now sleeping from 7.00 pm until 6.00 am every night.

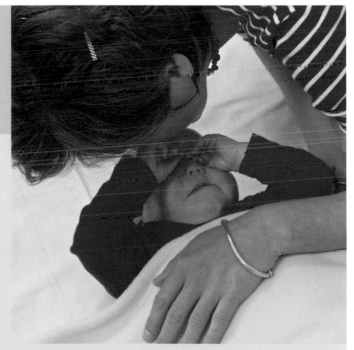

Steps

Step 1 Establish a good and consistent bedtime routine (see page 30, Creating a sleep routine).

Step 2 During week 1, if your child wakes and cries, wait 5 minutes before going into his room to reassure him and yourself that he is all right. Keep the visit brief and do not lift him up or cuddle him. Simply say: 'I am here, go to sleep' and leave. If he is still crying after 10 minutes, repeat the procedure, then again after 15 minutes if he is still crying. Repeat checking at 15-minute intervals until he is asleep.

Step 3 If your baby does not appear to be responding to controlled crying, check that you are not staying in the room too long, repositioning or touching

Resist the temptation to cuddle or lift your baby when applying the controlled-crying technique. Visits shoud be brief and unemotional.

your baby. Check, also, that you are leaving sufficient time between visits to his room. You may be disrupting your baby as he tries to settle himself by returning too quickly, and it may be necessary to increase the amount of time between visits.

You may even have to consider whether revisiting your baby is keeping him wake. If this is the case you may decide to leave him to completely settle himself and not visit the room at all.

Solution 7 Night waking 0–12 months

Try this plan if you have twins or siblings experiencing sleep problems at the same time.

? Problem

Adam and Ben were 10-month-old twins who had never slept through the night. Their parents were having to get up several times during the night to rock the boys back to sleep.

The twins had been born 6 weeks prematurely but were now growing well and healthily. Their 2-year-old sister was sleeping in the parents' room while the twins slept in the same bedroom in separate cots.

The family had a nanny who helped with the bedtime routine. Both boys used dummies and were rocked separately for 10–15 minutes until they fell asleep by about 7.30 pm. They would be woken around 10.00 pm, given a bottle of milk and a cuddle, and rocked back to sleep. They would then wake two or three times every night at around 2.00 am and 4.00 am – not always at the same time – and would be rocked back to sleep again. Their day started around 6.00 am. In the daytime they would nap for 1 hour in the morning and 1½ hours after lunch, on each occasion being rocked to sleep.

The mother was always worried about letting the twins cry at bedtime in case they woke their sister, who she also described as a 'difficult sleeper'.

Quote from parent *'We would like to be able to teach our twins to fall asleep by themselves and possibly sleep through the night.'*

Diagnosis

The bedtime routine was poorly structured: it took too long and was interrupted by having a feed and a play downstairs after bathtime. Both boys associated rocking and sucking a dummy with going to sleep.

Plan

The parents were instructed to set up a structured bedtime routine. They were to have their pre-bed milk downstairs before starting the bedtime routine, to begin to disassociate feeding with sleep. At 6.30 pm, the parents were to give the boys a bath, dress them for bed, lay them in their cots, say goodnight and leave the room. They were then to use the controlled-crying technique to teach the twins to settle by themselves. They were allowed to keep their dummies, but they were attached to their nightclothes so that the boys

could find them without disturbing their parents. Daytime naps were scheduled, with a 45-minute nap in the morning and a 1½-hour nap in the afternoon.

Results

Progress after 1 week was slow because their mother implemented the bedtime routine but continued to rock the twins to sleep. Neither boy was happy having milk before his bath so they were given some milk in the bedroom after the bath. Both boys were almost asleep drinking the milk. Their mother was advised to persevere with the original plan, and to move on to settling the babies using the controlled-crying technique.

After 1 night of controlled crying, both children settled well within 30 minutes at bedtime. Adam woke twice in the night and required a couple of visits into the room before he went back to sleep. Ben didn't wake.

By day 3, Adam was sleeping through to 6.00 am. Ben woke at 5.00 am and did not go back to sleep with controlled crying. The parents were advised to continue with the controlled crying at bedtime and, if necessary, during the night. If early morning waking continued, the parents were told not to go into the room at all, in case their visits were providing the boys with the incentive to keep awake at that time of the morning.

After a week of controlled crying, both Adam and Ben were settling at 6.45 pm and sleeping through to 6.30 am or 7.00 am. They were in their cots for daytime naps, but took 10–15 minutes of controlled crying to settle. At this stage, their mother was advised to stop using the controlled-crying technique for their daytime naps and simply to leave the boys to settle themselves.

Steps

Step 1 If you have twins, you need to deal with them together, aiming for them both to be asleep at the same time. Establish a set bedtime for them and create a simple routine that will suit both of them simultaneously (see page 30, Creating a sleep routine). Stick to it, tucking them both in at the same time, and don't worry about one waking the other: most twins do not seem bothered by each other's cries.

Step 2 If either or both babies cry, use the controlled-crying technique (see page 75). Apply the technique in exactly the same way as you would for a single child, visiting both at the same time if necessary.

Step 3 If your children use dummies and are old enough to replace them, attach them to their nightclothes using a special dummy clip, or place lots of dummies in the bed to help them find one more easily.

You can use controlled-crying to settle your child at nap times as well as at night-time.

Solution 8 Night waking 1–6 years

Try this gradual-retreat plan if, like Isobel, your child is over 1 year old, wakes in the night and refuses to go back to sleep unless certain factors are present.

? Problem

Isobel was 3 years old. Her mother was a housewife and her father worked long hours. Isobel's sleep problems began a year earlier when she had an ear infection and her parents had to go to her in the night.

Isobel would begin to get ready for bed at 6.45 pm and by 7.45 pm she would be asleep on her own in her room. However, she would wake crying two to three times on most nights.

Her parents would go to her room, replace her duvet and say: 'Go back to sleep, it's the middle of the night'. They would then lie on her bed until she was asleep. Isobel would go back to sleep quickly – until the next time she called out and the same thing happened.

Isobel's mother was constantly tired. She had suffered from postnatal depression and felt that the lack of sleep was making her symptoms worse. Both parents felt irritable and didn't know what to do to remedy the problem. Isobel was tired in the day, was prone to tantrums and she didn't eat well.

Diagnosis

Both parents had hoped Isobel would return to her usual sleep patterns once her ear infection cleared up, but her night waking had become habitual. She found the contact with her parents during the night comforting and reassuring. As long as her parents continued to offer comfort during the night, this behaviour was unlikely to change.

Plan

The aim was to stop Isobel waking at night and to decrease the interaction and reassurance she received from her parents. A gradual-retreat programme was used to teach Isobel to go back to sleep in the night with little intervention from her parents (see page 76). She was also rewarded for going back to sleep nicely (see page 83, Sleep fairy).

Results

Isobel woke three times during the first night. Her parents sat on her bed rather than lay with her and she didn't protest, because she was so taken with the idea of a reward from the sleep fairy. She went back to sleep quickly and received her reward in the morning.

On nights 7, 8 and 9 Isobel woke once only. Her parents continued with the plan and had now started to move away from the side of her bed. Progress continued and Isobel only really protested when the parent's chair was moved outside her door. Her parents refused to be drawn into the protest and ignored her behaviour. By night 3 of the chair being outside the room, Isobel had settled again and slept through the night.

For over 3 weeks, Isobel had woken only briefly: her murmurs were ignored and she had gone back to sleep by herself. Her parents had hardly been disturbed at night. They were very pleased, and the whole family felt better. Isobel was eating better, and everyone reported a much happier and more settled child.

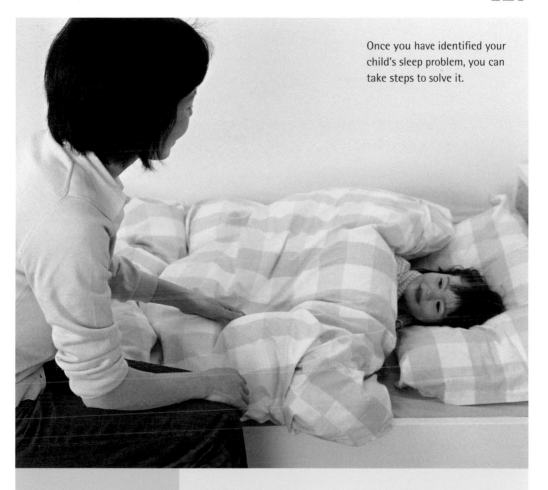

Once you have identified your child's sleep problem, you can take steps to solve it.

Steps

Step 1 If you have been lying with your child to go to sleep use a gradual-retreat programme, applying each of the steps for a maximum of 3 nights before moving on to the next (see page 74, Sleep-training techniques). Do not enter into a conversation with your child. Maintain minimum interaction, but use brief statements like 'Go to sleep and I will sit here with you'. Every time your child wakes in the night, maintain consistency and do the same thing each time.

Step 2 If your child is old enough, you can use a reward system for her going back to sleep without a fuss (see page 82, Positive reinforcement – rewards).

Step 3 Once she is asleep, always remember to wait 10 minutes before leaving the room, to be sure that she is in deep sleep.

Step 4 If your child makes a fuss, ignore her or leave the room, shutting the door briefly. Return after 10-20 seconds, resume your position and continue as before. You may have to leave a number of times before your child settles without a fuss (see page 87, What if...?).

Solution 9 Night waking 1–6 years

Try this gradual-retreat plan if, like Molly, your child keeps getting out of bed during the night and coming to find you, or calling to you from her room.

Problem

Molly was 18 months old and had no siblings. She had never slept through the night and had cried a lot since birth. Cranial treatments at 6 months improved the crying, but didn't solve her sleep problem. Molly slept in a bed in her own room.

Molly's evening routine started at 6.45 pm with a bath. She would then come back downstairs at 7.30 pm and sit on the sofa with her mother and father, drinking her milk and falling asleep. She would then be taken to bed, already asleep, at 8.00–8.30 pm. If she was unable to get to sleep on the sofa, Molly would fall asleep in bed with her parents at 9.30 pm.

She would wake every night at about 12.30 am, walk to her parents' room and get into their bed. She would sleep there until morning and wake at about 7.30 am. In the day she slept for about an hour, usually on a parent's lap on the sofa.

Molly's parents had tried to take her to bed when sleepy but she would wake up and completely revive, as if she had never been tired.

Diagnosis

Molly had learned to go to sleep in specific conditions – on the sofa and with her parents – so she needed these same conditions to be present when she roused during the night. She slept through happily once she was in her parents' bed, which reinforced the need for their presence.

Plan

Molly needed a more focused bedtime routine so that she stayed in the bedroom area once the routine had started. The aim for week 1 was for Molly to fall asleep in her own bed and stay there all night. Her parents sat with her until she fell asleep. If she woke and tried to get into her parents' bed she was guided back to her bed, and sat with again until she went back to sleep.

Results

Molly responded well to the new bedtime routine and fell asleep each night in her own bed. On night 1 she took an hour to go to sleep. On night 2 she took 25 minutes to go to sleep but, by night 3, she was taking 15 minutes to go to sleep. During the night she woke twice on nights 1 and 2. On night 3 she woke three times to test her parents resolve, but they remained consistent. As the week went on, she woke just once a night.

Molly's parents began the gradual-retreat process, moving the chair closer to the bedroom door every fourth night until it was outside the room. They repeated the same process if she woke during the night. They were surprised how well she responded to the gradual retreat. She continued to settle well at bedtime and even though she woke once during the night for the first week, she took less and less time to go back to sleep. By the third week Molly was occasionally making a brief sound, to which her parents didn't feel they needed to respond: they knew they could leave her to get back to sleep.

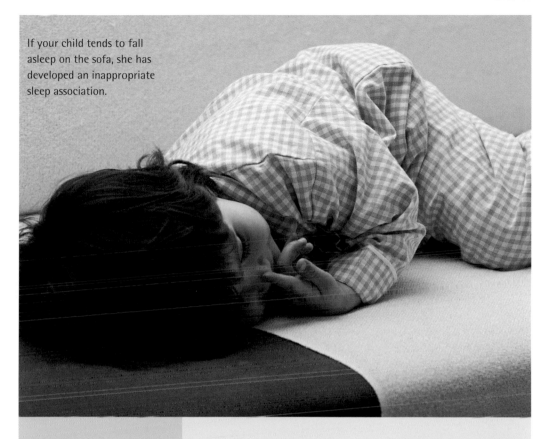

If your child tends to fall asleep on the sofa, she has developed an inappropriate sleep association.

Steps

Step 1 Make sure your child has a focused and calming bedtime routine (see page 30, Creating a sleep routine). It should take no longer than 45 minutes and should happen in the bedroom area. If your child needs you or other 'props' to get her to sleep at bedtime, she has developed inappropriate sleep associations (see page 53).

For week 1 of the programme you need to concentrate on applying the bedtime routine and getting your child to fall asleep in her bed at bedtime and stay in her own bed all night. You will sit with her as she does so only leaving once you know she is asleep.

Step 2 Each time your child wakes during the night, guide her back to her room, not carrying her or picking her up. Keep interaction to a minimum, giving simple, clear commands. Then sit on the chair and repeat as at bedtime. Once she is asleep wait an extra 10 minutes before leaving her room to be sure she is in a deep sleep.

Step 3 From week 2, now that you have established the bedtime routine and ensured your child goes to sleep and stays in her own bed all night, you can start the gradual-retreat programme. (see page 74, Sleep-training techniques). As your child achieves the gradual-retreat stages, reward her with plenty of praise in the morning.

Solution 10 Night waking 1–6 years

Try this combined gradual-retreat and reward plan if, like Peter, your child is over 3 years old and is waking in the night after moving into a bed.

Problem

?

Three-year-old Peter had slept through the night from the age of 5 weeks until moving into a bed at the age of 2 years 3 months. Periods of night waking began and grew progressively worse with time.

On a typical night, Peter's mother would sit with him while he went off to sleep – or would leave the room when he was very sleepy – and Peter would wake four times during the night. He had a dummy attached to his favourite teddy, which he always seemed to find when he woke, but he would often come into his parents' room in the middle of the night and needed to be led back to his own bed and tucked in again. His parents allowed him to come into their bed after 6.00 am. He had one daytime nap on the sofa, which lasted an hour.

The sleep problem seemed to affect all aspects of family life. Peter's parents had no time for each other and felt a strain on their relationship. Peter's behaviour in the daytime was also difficult to cope with, because he was over-tired. He would become very aggressive, kicking and hitting out at his parents.

Quote from mother *'I was pregnant at the time, and suffering with antenatal depression. Sleep deprivation contributed to this.'*

Diagnosis

Moving into a 'big' bed had created sleep problems. Peter needed a parent with him to settle at bedtime, otherwise, he would get out of bed. This learned association also affected his ability to return to sleep in the night without a 'quick fix' from his mother. Peter also wanted to get into his parents' bed and woke frequently, hoping to join them.

Plan

Peter's parents needed to teach him to go to sleep alone at bedtime and to be able to go back to sleep when he woke in the night. He also needed to be taught to recognize 'wake-up time' and to know when it was acceptable to go into his parents' room.

A routine was set for a 7.00 pm bedtime: at 6.00 pm Peter had his last milk/snack downstairs, before starting a relaxing bedtime routine at 6.15 pm, with Peter in bed by 7.00 pm. His parents applied a gradual-retreat programme, with a reward from the sleep fairy for going to bed nicely at bedtime. A lamp attached to a timer switch was set to come on when it was appropriate for Peter to get up. A daytime nap of 1 hour was set for after lunch, to avoid napping after 3.00 pm.

Results

Peter's mother had progressed to the door within 9 days of starting the gradual-retreat programme. Peter was settling quickly but still woke four times in the night. The lamp was timed to come on at 6.30 am but hadn't had much effect as Peter was still waking and coming into his parents' room through the night.

The gradual-retreat programme progressed until Peter's mother was outside the door when he went to sleep, but Peter continued to wake in the night. His mother was advised to lead Peter back to his bedroom door but not to go into the room herself. Instead she was to sit on her chair outside the room. Furthermore Peter was now only going to be rewarded if he went to bed nicely and didn't get out of bed until the lamp was on in the morning. The lamp was set to come on earlier than his average wake-up time of 5.45 am to give him a chance to achieve this.

Peter coped well and understood the concept of waiting for the light to come on before waking his parents. He woke once a night but stopped getting out of bed and called for his mother instead.

A week on and the goal posts for the reward system were changed again, and Peter received a reward if he didn't get out of bed or call out before the lamp was on. A week later he was consistently sleeping from 7.00 pm–7.00 am. The whole process took one month.

Encourage your child to engage in quiet activities in the hour before bedtime.

Steps

Step 1 Establish a regular bedtime, avoid stimulating activities in the hour before bedtime and stick to a set bedtime routine (see page 30, Creating a sleep routine).

Step 2 Try a gradual-retreat programme to teach your child to settle alone at bedtime and to go back to sleep during the night. (See page 74, Sleep-training techniques). If your child is old enough, use the retreat programme in conjunction with a reward system. The sleep fairy can be very motivating for young children and helps to reinforce the positive behavioural changes you are making. (See page 82, Positive reinforcement – rewards).

Step 3 If your child has difficulty knowing when it is time to get up in the morning, provide him with a small lamp attached to a timer switch. Set it to come on 15 minutes before his usual waking time, which will give him a chance to achieve the goal you have set straight away. To be successful you must make sure your child understands the system.

Step 4 Despite making good progress with the programme, your child may still be waking at night. If this is the case, you may be inadvertently rewarding your child with too much interaction when he wakes. Make sure all contact is minimal, and that you are using clear but simple commands. Finally, it may be that your child will only sleep through the night once you have fully completed the programme and are out of his room.

Solution 11 Night waking 1–6 years

Try this plan if, like Amanda, your child is awake for long periods in the night and needs your presence to go back to sleep.

Problem

Amanda was 3 years 8 months old. For the past year had been coming into her parents' bed since returning from a holiday, when the family shared a room.

At 6.30 pm Amanda would have a bath, then come downstairs for milk and her favourite television programme. She was then taken to bed and one parent would sit with her while she fell asleep. She was usually asleep by 8.30 pm.

Amanda would wake about four times every night, calling out and crying. She sometimes came into her parents' room and bed and then one of her parents would carry her back to her own room and get into bed with her. She had a 10-month-old baby brother, who woke at night and had milk to get back to sleep. Her parents were worried that Amanda's crying would disturb him further.

Diagnosis

Amanda's bedtime routine was not focused and she would get a second wind at bedtime and find it very difficult to go to sleep. She needed her parents presence at bedtime for both reassurance and as a sleep prop, as she had developed inappropriate sleep associations.

To focus the bedtime routine it was important that it took no longer than 45 minutes. Once started, there was no return to the living area; and that it left her calm and ready to sleep. She also needed to learn to fall asleep without the presence of her parents.

Plan

Amanda's bedtime routine was to start with her pre-bed milk downstairs, at 6.30 pm. She would then go up for her bath and get straight into bed for one or two stories, with lights out at 7.15 pm. Amanda's parents started a seven-step gradual-retreat programme. They wanted to be able to put Amanda and her brother into bed while they were awake and for them to sleep uninterrupted through the night. Motivation for Amanda was provided by rewards from the sleep fairy.

Results

Amanda adjusted quickly to the new routine and was asleep within 15 minutes of saying 'goodnight'. On nights 1 and 2, she asked one of her parents to lie down on her bed. They kept interaction brief, saying: 'Amanda, go to sleep, I will stay with you,' and did not give in to her request. She responded well to the consistent, clear boundaries.

On night 1, she woke crying at 1.00 am, but her mother sat on her bed and waited for her to go back to sleep. She did so after an hour and slept through until 6.30 am. This pattern was repeated for 3 nights. During week 1, Amanda wanted to get back into her parents' bed just once, but realized from their firm response that she was not going to achieve this. Also, she loved the sleep fairy and wanted to get her reward in the morning.

After 2 weeks, the parents were able to put Amanda to bed and sit outside her door as she went to sleep. She had stopped waking in the night and slept for 11 hours. The sleep fairy was still visiting. The parents felt less tired and able to go out in the evening. Amanda was happier during the day, with fewer tantrums and her appetite had improved.

Avoid allowing your child to sleep with you in your bed.

Steps

Step 1 Keep a sleep diary for one week so you can compare your progress (see page 72, Keeping a sleep diary). If your child still has daytime naps, check that they are not too long or too late for your child's age, and adjust them accordingly (see page 17, Sleep needs).

Step 2 Start a gradual-retreat plan, keeping any interaction to a minimum (see page 74, Sleep-training techniques). Do this at bedtime and every time she wakes in the night. If she gets out of bed, do not pick her up but simply guide her back. Once asleep, always wait 10 minutes before leaving the room to make sure that she is in a deep sleep.

Step 3 Do not let your child get into your bed in the night. You must be consistent here, or your child will become confused. It may be difficult for her to go back to sleep early in the morning at first, so you may need to be flexible about wake-up time.

Step 4 Once you no longer need to sit outside the door, tell your child you will be in your bedroom tidying up as she goes to sleep. Never say you will return in a minute as she may wait for you, or wake later in the night and wonder where you are. Do this for 2–3 nights.

Now tell her you are going downstairs to make supper: she will like to imagine you doing something as she falls asleep. Again do this for 2–3 nights.

Step 5 You can use a reward system such as the sleep fairy to help encourage your child to make these changes (see page 82, Positive reinforcement – rewards).

Solution 12 Night waking 1–6 years

Try this plan if one of your children is disturbing the other with her sleep problem.

?
Problem

At the age of nearly 3 years, Louise's night-time crying was greatly disturbing that of her sister Hannah, age 5, with whom she had shared a room since she was 5 months old.

Quote from mother
'We knew what we had to do really, but the dilemma of disrupting Hannah's sleep was too much. No one had told us that this problem could be sorted out more gently.'

Louise's bedtime routine almost always ran smoothly. She and her sister would be given a bath and then be taken into their bedroom for stories on Louise's bed. Then both children would be tucked into bed and usually went to sleep as soon as their parent left the room.

Louise's sleep problems started when she was almost 3 years old, and made the move from a cot-bed to a bed. Now she would come into her parents' bedroom three or four times during the night. After several visits, her parents would eventually give in and allow her into their bed. Her sister Hannah would generally stay asleep.

Louise's mother was shocked by the sudden development of a sleep problem after nearly 2 years of sleeping through the night. She also felt very restricted in the things she could try because the children shared a bedroom. Taking Louise into the parents' bed was mainly to avoid disturbing Hannah.

After 10 weeks of taking Louise into their bed, the parents decided to try to solve the problem using controlled crying. This woke Hannah, who became so upset that her father had to sit with her for some time to calm her down. After a few days, Hannah also asked to get into the parents' bed. They resisted this request, but struggled to calm her down.

Louise's parents persevered for 1 week – getting nowhere with their attempt at controlled crying – at which point they decided to seek help.

Diagnosis

Louise had a night-waking problem, which was being sustained by the reward of coming into her parents' bed. The controlled-crying technique used to try and solve this problem affected Hannah's sleep causing her increased anxiety and tiredness.

Plan

The plan was to teach Louise to stay in her own bed all night and not come out of the room. This required a programme that would cause the least amount of disruption to her sister while allowing both children to continue sleeping in the same room. The preferred

approach was gradual retreat. The parents explained clearly to Hannah that they were teaching Louise to be able to go back to sleep in the night by herself and although they were going to sit in the bedroom, they expected Hannah to go back to sleep nicely if she was disturbed. If she did so, she was rewarded by the sleep fairy. Louise was rewarded by the sleep fairy for going back to sleep nicely in her own bed during the night.

Results

Louise responded to the programme almost immediately. She made some requests to get into her parents' bed initially but, once she realized that they were not going to give in, she stopped asking. She seemed to trust very early on that her parents were going to sit with her while she went back to sleep.

The first few nights she woke three times and took around half an hour to go back to sleep. As the gradual-retreat programme progressed, Louise woke only once a night and returned to sleep quickly. Hannah was not stirring at all. Both children were highly motivated by the sleep fairy and loved to compare their gifts in the morning.

Within 2 weeks of starting the programme, the parents had managed to get outside the bedroom door. Louise continued to wake once for a couple of nights but was easily reassured from a distance.

Steps

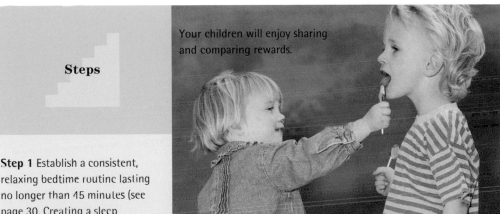

Your children will enjoy sharing and comparing rewards.

Step 1 Establish a consistent, relaxing bedtime routine lasting no longer than 45 minutes (see page 30, Creating a sleep routine). If your children are old enough, explain clearly the new bedtime 'rules' and what you expect of them.

Step 2 If you have two children sharing a bedroom and one of those has a sleep problem, a gradual-retreat programme is the most appropriate technique to choose (see page 74, Sleep-training techniques). This technique does not involve leaving your child to cry, so the sibling is less likely to be disturbed. He will be reassured that you are dealing with his brother or sister and will go back to sleep, leaving you to it. Gradually distancing yourself from the child with the sleep problem will give that child time to adjust to the changes you are making without upsetting them.

If your child has a well-established bedtime routine and has always settled alone without your presence, you do not need to make any changes at bedtime. You should continue settling your child as before and only use the retreat method for night waking.

If your child has not needed you to stay in the room after taking him back to bed in the night you can start step 1 of the gradual-retreat progamme sitting on a chair/cushion a small distance from the bed. You can then continue with the next stages of the programme.

Step 3 If you set up a reward system for the child who has difficulty sleeping you should think about setting up a reward system for the 'good' sleeper too. Recognizing positive behaviour will help to maintain good sleep habits as your children grow older.

Solution 13 Night feeding
0–6 months

Try this plan if, like James, your baby wakes for frequent night feeds and needs physical contact, such as a cuddle or rocking, to go to sleep.

Problem

James was 5 months old, with no siblings. He slept in a cot next to his mother and would wake frequently for feeds. His father slept in the spare room.

James had cried a lot since birth, and his parents found it very difficult to settle him. He didn't like being put down in his cot, so spent most of the day and evening on his mother's lap. He was colicky for a while, especially in the evenings.

He went to sleep on the breast and was transferred to his cot at bedtime. He woke four or five times every night, and each time the process was repeated. In the day, while mostly falling asleep on the breast, he occasionally fell asleep in the car or in his pushchair. James was often very fractious and appeared very tired, but would only have two to three brief naps.

Fatigue and frustration made his mother tearful and his father irritable. They knew he could not settle himself but did not know how to help him.

Diagnosis

James was unable to fall asleep by himself. He was having too many night feeds for his age and suffered from a lack of a regular routine, both at bedtime and during the day.

Plan

After establishing a regular bedtime schedule, the plan was to start a gradual-retreat programme to teach James to fall asleep by himself, aiming for him to be asleep by about 7.30 pm.

Results

James's first night went well. His last breast-feed was given prior to starting the bedtime routine, then he was rocked to sleep within 20 minutes. He woke a couple of times in the early evening but his parents managed to rock him back to sleep quickly each time.

His feed times were set for 10.30 pm, 1.00 am and 4.00 am. If he woke and a feed was not due or he was

difficult to settle after a feed, his parents applied the gradual-retreat programme. He woke at 6.00 am. His daytime naps were scheduled according to his age and he was settled as at night. Both parents saw a dramatic change in James after only 24 hours.

James was a little unsettled at the beginning of each new stage of retreat but he quickly adapted. He seemed much happier during the day and his daytime naps were better spaced and longer.

James's parents made sure his daytime milk feeds compensated for the drop in night feeding. At the end of week 3, they were no longer touching him as he went to sleep or if he woke in the night. He had stopped waking in the early evening and slept well, from settling at 7.30 pm until the first feed at around 11.00 pm. His parents felt much more in control.

James occasionally woke between feeds but managed to resettle himself quickly. His parents were now considering moving him into his own room so that his father could at last come back to his own bed.

Steps

Retreat programme	
Nights	**Activity**
1–3	Rock your baby to sleep. Once asleep, wait 10 minutes before placing him in the cot to ensure he is in a deep sleep
4–6	Hold your baby in your arms with no rocking motion until he is asleep
7–9	Start settling your baby in the cot. Cuddle your baby in his cot
10–12	Stop cuddling and pat your baby to sleep
13–15	Stroke your baby to sleep
16–18	Hold your baby's hand while sitting by the cot
19–20	Sit by the side of the cot on a chair or a cushion but not touching your baby

Step 1 Establish an early evening routine. Start with a bedtime feed but do not let your baby fall asleep at this time. Give her a bath, get her into nightclothes and into her own room (see page 30, Creating a sleep routine).

Step 2 If your baby has been fed or cuddled to sleep, start the gradual-retreat programme above. This one is scheduled to last 3 weeks (see also page 74, Sleep-training techniques).

Always wait 10 minutes after your baby is asleep before attempting to leave her. Keep other interaction, including eye contact, to a minimum.

Whenever your baby wakes during the night, use the same gradual-retreat process as at bedtime, unless it is a feeding time.

Step 3
Space feeds to work alongside the gradual-retreat programme. After 3 nights of 3-hourly feeds, increase the interval between feeds to 3½ hours (see page 75, Schedule for reducing or spacing feeds). Repeat this for 3 nights while you move on to the next stage: holding your baby in your arms until asleep.

You can continue to increase the spacing between feeds, even slowing the rate down to weekly time changes, as you feel your baby's requirements for night feeds is decreasing. Eventually you will be able to phase out all the night feeds.

Feeding schedule	
First feed	Not before 10.00 pm
Second feed	No less than 3 hours later
Third feed	No less than 3 hours from last feed
Wake-up feed	At 6.30–7.00 am

Step 4 Make sure that your baby has one nap a day in her cot; the remaining naps can be in the car or pushchair. Use the gradual-retreat method to get her to sleep. Try to avoid your baby falling asleep feeding – aiming to feed after a nap rather than before it will help this (see page 34, Number and length of naps).

Try to avoid your baby falling asleep during daytime feeds.

Solution 14 Night feeding over 6 months

Try this controlled-crying plan if, like Aidan, your child is over 6 months old and wakes for small, frequent, night feeds.

Problem

Aidan was 8 months old with no siblings, and slept in a cot in his parents' room. He fell asleep on the breast at bedtime and needed the breast to go back to sleep in the night.

Aidan was a very colicky baby and had been seen several times by a paediatrician for persistent crying and discomfort after feeding. He was very windy and often impossible to settle, suggesting mild reflux.

Aidan's bedtime routine consisted of supper at 6.00 pm, followed by playtime and a bath. He was then usually breast-fed to sleep. His mother would try a dummy if he had difficulties settling, which could take up to 20 minutes.

He woke two to four times every night. If he failed to settle with a dummy, he was breast-fed back to sleep. Significantly, these feeds were often very short, lasting only 2–3 minutes. Aidan would then come into his parents' bed from about 4.30 am, by which time they were desperate for sleep.

Aidan's daytime naps were a little erratic. He usually settled with a dummy but could take hours to go to sleep.

Quote from mother *'Aidan will have three brilliant days when we think "this is it, he has cracked it". And then we will have four awful days when he is irritable, jumpy, frantic, tearful and cannot be put down or get to sleep or stay asleep during the night. We are quite concerned and close to our physical limits.'*

Diagnosis

Aidan's history of colic and reflux had prevented his parents establishing a good sleep routine. While being put to the breast for feeds and comfort as a new-born had helped calm this irritable baby, it had also caused him to associate breast-feeding with sleep, consequently preventing him from self-settling at bedtime and in the night.

Plan

The objective was to teach Aidan to settle without breast-feeding. He had his pre-bed feed before his parents started the bedtime routine, and rather than

falling asleep on the breast or dummy he would learn to settle himself using a controlled-crying technique. More structure was given to his night-feeding schedule by limiting his night feeds, and gradually weaning him off them altogether. He was not offered a feed before 2.00 am and then not again until after 6.00 am. Aidan was not to come into his parents' bed to sleep at night, further reducing his incentive to wake.

Results

Just 3 days after starting the programme Aidan was already settling well in his own bed. This took 40 minutes of controlled crying on the first night, decreasing to 10 minutes by the third night. On the third night, his parents did not have to go back into his bedroom after saying goodnight to Aidan at bedtime. He woke for a breast-feed around 5.00 am, settling immediately afterwards and sleeping through to the morning.

By the end of week 1, Aidan had slept through the night on two occasions. There was then a setback because he developed a viral infection and his parents had to attend to him in the night when he woke. He began to sleep through again as soon as he had recovered. He continued to nap well in the daytime – he was not being breast-fed to sleep at all, and he settled alone in his cot.

Because Aidan was taking very little milk during the night at the start of the second week his mother was advised not to breast-feed at all during the night, but to feed at any time after 6.00 am. The ease of dropping the night feeds confirmed this was truly a sleep association problem.

Within 10 days Aidan was sleeping through the night, and his daytime routine was excellent.

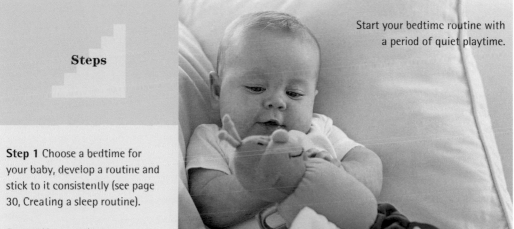

Start your bedtime routine with a period of quiet playtime.

Steps

Step 1 Choose a bedtime for your baby, develop a routine and stick to it consistently (see page 30, Creating a sleep routine).

Step 2 If your baby has been reliant on breast-feeding to sleep, begin to take milk out of his routine by offering his pre-bed feed downstairs before starting the bedtime routine. This should be a calm, quiet time but not a sleepy feed – you do not want him to fall asleep.

Step 3 Once you have put your baby in the cot, say goodnight. You then need to follow your preferred choice of technique (see page 74, Sleep-training techniques). If using controlled crying, be sure not to touch your baby when visiting the room.

If your child stands in the cot do not be tempted to lay him down (see page 84, What if...?). If you are concerned your baby is cold, use a sleeping bag or 'layer' him up rather than tuck him in every time you go into the room. The slightest contact from you may encourage your baby to stay awake.

Step 4 When your child is ill, you have to do whatever is necessary to help him get better. But you should also try to avoid 'going backwards' as regards his sleep habits if at all possible. Above all, go back to your programme of sleep improvement as soon as your child has recovered (see page 47, Illness).

Solution 15 Night feeding over 6 months

Try this plan if, like Charles, your child is over 6 months and wakes for frequent night feeds.

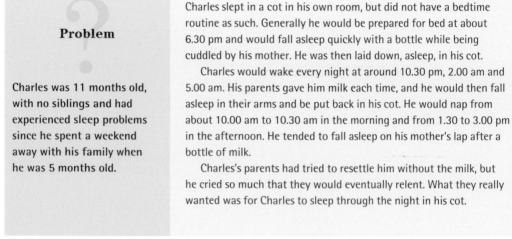

Problem

Charles was 11 months old, with no siblings and had experienced sleep problems since he spent a weekend away with his family when he was 5 months old.

Charles slept in a cot in his own room, but did not have a bedtime routine as such. Generally he would be prepared for bed at about 6.30 pm and would fall asleep quickly with a bottle while being cuddled by his mother. He was then laid down, asleep, in his cot.

Charles would wake every night at around 10.30 pm, 2.00 am and 5.00 am. His parents gave him milk each time, and he would then fall asleep in their arms and be put back in his cot. He would nap from about 10.00 am to 10.30 am in the morning and from 1.30 to 3.00 pm in the afternoon. He tended to fall asleep on his mother's lap after a bottle of milk.

Charles's parents had tried to resettle him without the milk, but he cried so much that they would eventually relent. What they really wanted was for Charles to sleep through the night in his cot.

Diagnosis

Charles's problems arose because he had inappropriately associated sucking with going to sleep. Consequently, when he entered a light sleep phase during the night he would depend on a milk feed and a cuddle to get back to sleep. Because he was taking a large volume of milk during the night, he had learned to be hungry at night. In fact, he was still on a very young baby's night-feeding schedule and no longer needed these feeds. Rather than helping him to sleep, these feeds had now become the reason he woke.

Plan

Charles was given his pre-bed milk before his parents started getting him ready for bed, in order to end the association of this feed with bedtime, and his parents established a relaxing and focused bedtime routine. Charles was taught how to settle himself to sleep using a gradual-retreat programme. Finally a schedule for reducing feeds was set up to wean Charles off his night-time milk.

Results

Nights 1-3 were very hard work for Charles's parents, especially at bedtime, as he was very upset. Even with the gradual-retreat programme, he took a long time to go to sleep. They persevered in reducing the amount of milk they offered him every night by ½ fl oz (15 ml) each feed. However things almost hit crisis point when the volume reached 3 fl oz (90 ml) because Charles found it very difficult to get back to sleep on such a small amount of milk. The parents' hard work eventually paid off, however, and once over this last hurdle, things went smoothly and they were able to stop the feeds completely. With consistency and perseverance from his parents Charles was settling into the routine instigated by the gradual-retreat programme. He began to gain the ability to self-settle at bedtime and, once the night feeds stopped, if he woke during the night.

With gradual retreat, it is important for your child to be put to bed asleep before you leave the room.

Steps

Step 1 Choose a bedtime for your child and stick to it. Make sure you establish a relaxing and consistent bedtime routine. (See page 30, Creating a sleep routine). Give your baby his last feed in the living room. This will disassociate sleeping from feeding and sucking (see page 53, Inappropriate sleep associations). He should be offered a full feed at this time. Do not let your child fall asleep on the feed.

Step 2 If your baby had previously settled by feeding to sleep in your arms, you can teach him to self-settle using the gradual-retreat programme (see page 76).

Step 3 During the night, aim to decrease the amount of milk by $1/2$–1 fl oz (15–30 ml) every night. If you are breast-feeding this is equivalent to $1/2$–1 minute breast-feeding. Do this for each feed (see page 74, Night feed weaning).

Solution 16 **Night feeding over 6 months**

Try this plan if, like Harry, your child is over 6 months old, settles alone, but wakes for frequent night feeds.

Problem

Harry was 8 months old, with a 3-year-old sister. He was a poor daytime feeder and slow to take solids, which meant he continued to wake up for large feeds of 8 fl oz (240 ml) two to three times a night.

Until the age of 3 months, Harry had always settled well, falling asleep while feeding at the breast. However, as his mother had some sleep and settling problems with his sister at the time, she was determined not to have them with Harry and decided to teach him to fall asleep by himself. She introduced a bedtime routine from 3 months that meant he was always put down in his cot awake and since then he happily went to sleep on his own.

However, at 8 months, Harry was still waking for night-time feeds. When his mother tried to reduce or stop these night-time feeds, Harry simply woke more frequently. His mother was tired with a toddler as well as a baby, so she had decided to keep the feeds going. She also thought that, as Harry was a bad daytime feeder, he was at least getting some nourishment at night.

Quote from mother *'I am now very tired and want a full night's sleep. I realize that to get Harry eating better in the day, he has to stop having night feeds.'*

Diagnosis

Harry did not have incorrect sleep associations but he did have a night-feeding problem. He had learned to feel hungry at night and, rather than resting, his body was having to produce enzymes to digest the 'food' he was taking. In fact, Harry had not moved on from the feeding schedule he had as a young baby. In taking such a large volume of milk at night, it was not surprising he was not hungry during the day.

Plan

The initial aim was to reduce Harry's night feeds gradually – to give his body a chance to adjust to the drop in milk volume – and then to stop these feeds altogether after about 10 days. The next aim was to use controlled crying to get Harry back to sleep if, as

suspected, he continued to wake at his usual feed time once the feeds had stopped. Harry's body clock was set to wake him up for feeds at regular times throughout the night.

Results

At the end of 10 days, Harry was no longer having milk at night. His daytime appetite had improved slowly, and within 2 weeks he was eating well. Harry's parents felt that their worst nights were in the middle of the programme, when Harry first noticed the drop in milk volume. However, after persevering with the controlled crying for 3 nights, things were now better than ever.

It was hard work, but his parents were very pleased they had been consistent with the programme. Everyone was sleeping much better now.

Steps

Step 1 Keep a sleep diary for a week to enable you to get a baseline from which to start your plan (see page 72). Check that your baby's daytime napping schedule is correct for his age (see page 32, Naps). Then make sure you have a good relaxing bedtime routine (see page 30, Creating a sleep routine).

Step 2 Aim to reduce each feed by 1 fl oz (30 ml) per night. If, after a few nights, you feel the milk is reducing too quickly for your baby, you can slow down this rate of reduction. For example, slow the reduction to 1 fl oz (30 ml) every other night. Once the feed has been reduced to 2 fl oz (60 ml) you can stop the night feeds altogether.

If you are breast-feeding your baby, use the same principles but reduce feeds by 1 minute a night (see page 75, Schedule for reducing or spacing feeds).

This gradual reduction of milk gives your baby's body a chance to adjust to the drop in volume. As the volume drops, your baby may have difficulty in getting back to sleep but this should only last for a few nights.

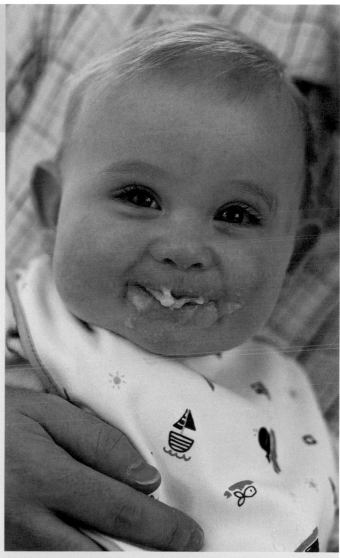

Use a feed-spacing schedule to reduce your baby's night feeds gradually.

Step 3 Use a sleep-training technique to get your baby back to sleep. Controlled-crying or gradual-retreat programmes are both suitable here and, if followed consistently, are very effective (see page 74, Sleep-training techniques).

As with any programme you may find that the first night is generally the worst, the second slightly better – while the third can be a test night. Persevere, and once past the test night your baby's sleep should start to settle down.

Solution 17 Night feeding over 6 months

Try this plan if, like Alice, your child is over 1 year old and still wakes often at night for milk.

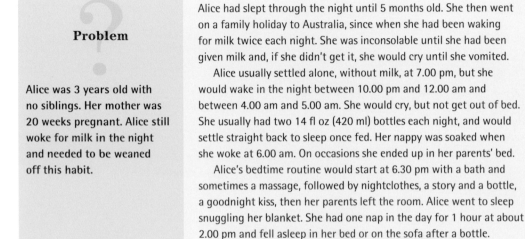

Problem

Alice was 3 years old with no siblings. Her mother was 20 weeks pregnant. Alice still woke for milk in the night and needed to be weaned off this habit.

Alice had slept through the night until 5 months old. She then went on a family holiday to Australia, since when she had been waking for milk twice each night. She was inconsolable until she had been given milk and, if she didn't get it, she would cry until she vomited.

Alice usually settled alone, without milk, at 7.00 pm, but she would wake in the night between 10.00 pm and 12.00 am and between 4.00 am and 5.00 am. She would cry, but not get out of bed. She usually had two 14 fl oz (420 ml) bottles each night, and would settle straight back to sleep once fed. Her nappy was soaked when she woke at 6.00 am. On occasions she ended up in her parents' bed.

Alice's bedtime routine would start at 6.30 pm with a bath and sometimes a massage, followed by nightclothes, a story and a bottle, a goodnight kiss, then her parents left the room. Alice went to sleep snuggling her blanket. She had one nap in the day for 1 hour at about 2.00 pm and fell asleep in her bed or on the sofa after a bottle.

Quote from mother *'I am getting more exhausted and irritable as my pregnancy progresses. We know Alice should sleep through the night, but we just can't seem to break the habit of her needing milk.'*

Diagnosis

Alice had a night-feeding problem. She associated having milk with going to sleep at bedtime and going back to sleep in the night. She was taking too large an amount of milk in the night for her age and, although she didn't need this milk she had 'learned' to be hungry. The large volume of fluid may also be causing her to wake more often with a full bladder.

Plan

The aim was to wean Alice off night feeds and teach her to resettle herself when she woke during the night. Her bedtime routine stayed the same, but she was given her milk prior to starting the routine. This ensured that she stopped associating milk with settling at bedtime.

Results

After 10 days, Alice was waking just once. The milk offered at night had been reduced gradually from a total of 14 fl oz (420 ml) to 1½ fl oz (45 ml) of milk. Finally, after offering 1 fl oz (30 ml) feeds for two nights, the night feeds were stopped altogether.

Alice needed several nights of gentle stroking when she woke, but her parents said goodnight and left the room before she settled. By day 16 of the programme Alice was sleeping right through.

Aim to gradually decrease the amount of milk offered until night feeds are eliminated.

Steps

Step 1 Offer pre-bed milk downstairs before starting your bedtime routine. If your child refuses pre-bed milk make sure she eats well during the day and try bringing her teatime forward a little if possible. She may then feel more like taking milk and, after a night or two, will settle into the new routine.

Step 2 Adopt a well-structured, relaxing bedtime routine lasting no more than 45 minutes (see page 30, Creating a sleep routine). If your child is unsettled at bedtime due to the change in routine, sit by the bed and stroke/pat or hold hands until your child is asleep but don't give her milk (see page 74, Sleep training techniques). You can teach your child new associations to get to sleep and go back to sleep in the night in conjunction with a weaning schedule (see page 75).

Step 3 Reduce the amount of milk offered in each bottle by 1 fl oz (30 ml) (or 1 minute on the breast) a night, starting with the amount your child has been accustomed to. When your child is taking 1 fl oz (30 ml) feeds (or on the breast for 1 minute) you can eliminate this feed altogether.

If, at any stage, you think your baby needs a little more time to adjust to the reduced amount of milk, slow down the reduction rate for 2–3 days and then continue with the schedule.

Solution 18 **Early rising**

Try this plan if, like Joshua, your child is aged between 3 and 6 years, waking early and appears tired and unable to cope with the day.

Problem

Joshua was 3 years old and had a 5-year-old brother. He had always been an early riser and was noisy when he woke up. By 3.00 pm he wanted to sleep, although his parents tried very hard not to let him. Joshua's behaviour was difficult at times and he had frequent tantrums.

Joshua had always fed at 5.00 am as a baby. But nearly 3 years on he still wanted an early drink of milk; he felt hungry at 5.00 am because he was accustomed to having his milk at this time. He drank the milk sitting downstairs with one of his parents, watching videos. This meant that a parent had to get up with him very early in the morning, sometimes 2 hours before his brother woke.

His parents had to go to bed early to cope with the early rising, and took shifts at the weekend to enable one of them to sleep in.

Joshua was clearly in need of more sleep. He had tantrums regularly and struggled to stay awake in the car, even on short journeys.

Quote from father *'We were just unable to cope with the early start any more and didn't understand why Joshua woke so early, especially as his brother slept until 7.00 am every day.'*

Diagnosis

Joshua's parents completed a sleep diary for a week, which showed that he had no trouble falling asleep by himself at bedtime and didn't wake during the night. However, he was sleep-deprived by at least an hour a day due to his early rising. He had built up a large sleep debt, which showed itself in his behaviour.

Joshua had learned to be hungry at 5.00 am from his baby days, so his body still required food at this time. He was also rewarded for early rising by one-to-one time with a parent and a video.

Plan

The aim was for Joshua to sleep for 11½ hours a night. A step-by-step programme was designed to give him guidance on when to get up and a reward system was introduced. Joshua's parents were asked to be patient with the programme because early rising is one of the most difficult sleep problems to solve and positive changes often take longer to achieve. They kept a sleep diary, recording the times Joshua woke, so they could see and monitor the changes themselves.

Joshua needed a way of knowing when it was appropriate for him to get up. As he was not old enough to tell the time, his parents decided to use a lamp with a timer. The aim was to teach him to stay in bed quietly until the lamp came on each morning, for which he would be rewarded.

What Joshua didn't know was that the time would be adjusted slowly, so that he stayed in bed longer and longer over a period of a few weeks, until he was staying in bed until about 7.00 am, like his brother.

The plan was to make slow and steady progress so that Joshua's body clock could adjust to having more night-time sleep.

Results

This gradual process taught Joshua to stay in his bed and, even if he woke, to drift back to sleep by resting quietly. Within a matter of weeks Joshua's body clock had readjusted and he was able to sleep through to an acceptable waking time. The tantrums had almost stopped, he no longer fell asleep in the car and his parents had time together in the evening again.

Encourage an early riser to stay quietly in his bedroom.

Steps

Step 1 If you have a child who settles and sleeps well but wakes too early, use a lamp with a low-wattage bulb and connect it to a timer switch (see page 82, Man-made sunrise). Any small lamp will do as long as your child can see it clearly from his bed but it is not close enough to wake him. Complete a sleep diary for a week leading up to the start of your programme to enable you to work out what time you need to set the lamp to come on (see page 72, Keeping a sleep diary).

Step 2 On the day that you put the plan into action, explain to your child that he should only get out of bed if the lamp is on. If not, he should try to go back to sleep or stay quietly in bed until the lamp comes on. You can use a reward system to encourage your child (see page 82).

During week 1, set the lamp to come on 15 minutes before your child's usual waking time, for example, at 5.15 am if he wakes at 5.30 am. Then, at this time, the lamp will already be on and he will receive his reward straight away. If he sleeps later, the lamp is not bright enough to wake him. Set the lamp to come on 15 minutes later the next week, and again the week after.

Continue to reset the timer on the lamp each week, until you have reached your goal, that is, the waking time that is appropriate for your child's age.

Step 3 It is important for you or your partner to get up when your child wakes and start the day with him as usual. The rest of the day needs to be structured as normal.

Solution 19 Late sleeping

Try this plan if, like Will, your child sleeps well, but at the wrong times, settling very late in the evening, sleeping through the night and waking late in the morning.

Problem

Will was almost 6 years old with an older brother. After being put to bed at night in his own room, he would often come downstairs saying he couldn't sleep, and end up going to sleep very late.

Will had had sleep problems from birth. He would start getting ready for bed at 8.00 pm. One of his parents would go up with him to get his bedroom ready and read him a story for 15–20 minutes. He or she would then say goodnight and close the bedroom door.

Will would then get up a number of times and come downstairs, saying he couldn't sleep. Eventually he would go to sleep alone in his own bed, but not until 10.00–12.00 pm. His parents would have great difficulty waking him every morning at 8.00 am and he would be tired and grumpy. At weekends he would naturally sleep until 9.00 am, occasionally until 10.00 am or 10.30 am. He also at times sleep-walked.

Will was sleep-deprived, which resulted in him getting into fights at school and made him tearful. His parents felt this was not in his nature. They had tried everything they could think of but all without success.

Quote from mother *'We wanted Will to settle to sleep without hours of delaying tactics'.*

Diagnosis

Keeping a sleep diary indicated that Will had a late sleep phase problem. He also had a sleep deficit, which was contributing to his sleep-walking at night and his moods during the day. He needed about 10½ hours sleep each night and was currently only having around 8 or 9 hours.

Plan

The plan was to use a late sleep phase programme, based on Will going to bed at the time he naturally fell asleep, however late this may be. Once he was able to fall asleep within 15–20 minutes of 'lights out', his bedtime was gradually moved forward in 15-minute stages. By moving the clock forward slowly, both Will and his body clock had time to adjust to the earlier sleep time.

As for all sleep programmes it was vital that Will's parents ensured he had a relaxing bedtime routine lasting no longer than 30–45 minutes.

Results

To begin with Will was even more tired because he was woken up every morning including weekends. (An important factor in keeping the plan on track – some children catch up on their sleep deficit at the weekend enabling them to go to sleep late again by Monday night. Failure to wake them at the weekend could jeopardize the whole plan.) Will responded very well to the programme and was falling asleep each night within 15 minutes.

Will's late sleep phase problem was well established, so the programme was adjusted to enable his body clock to shift slowly to a more appropriate sleeping time. Changes to the bedtimes were made weekly.

After 2 months, Will was asleep most nights by 8.30 pm – sometimes by 9.00 pm, but no later. As he had caught up on his sleep deficit he was no longer sleep-walking and he was a happier, less moody child. School fights had stopped.

Steps

Step 1 If, like Will, your child has a late sleep phase problem and naturally falls asleep too late for his age most nights, you need to shift his bedtime and sleep times according to the following schedule (see also page 79, Resetting your child's body clock).

Continue this progression until your child falls asleep at the desired time. Remember to succeed you must wake your child at a regular time each day, including weekends.

For a child with a deep-rooted late sleep problem, you may have more success if the adjustments to the bedtimes are made once a week.

Once your child's body clock has adjusted he will be better balanced emotionally.

Sleeping schedules			
Day	Start routine	Lights out	Aim to be asleep by
1–3	10.15 pm	10.45 pm	11.00 pm
4–6	10.00 pm	10.30 pm	10.45 pm
7–9	09.45 pm	10.15 pm	10.30 pm
Next 7 days	09.30 pm	10.00 pm	10.15 pm
Next 7 days	09.15 pm	09.45 pm	10.00 pm *

* Note: You will need to continue with this process until your child is asleep at the desired time.

Solution 20 Nightmares and night terrors

Try this plan if, like George, your child appears frightened by dreams or wakes at night confused and disoriented.

? Problem

George was 6 years old and had a 3-year-old sister. He had suffered from sleep problems as a young baby, had difficulties settling and often woke screaming or shouting a couple hours after going to sleep.

Quote from parent 'We can't understand why George's sleep-walking and shouting happens so frequently. It's like having a new baby again, being woken every night.'

George had boundless energy and seemed to 'survive' on a lot less sleep than other children of the same age – until the age of 3 he had woken daily at 5.00 am. It was when George's parents moved him into a bunk bed at 6 years that he started to sleep-walk and to scream and shout out. This was always about 2 hours after going to sleep. He appeared to be 'locked' into a dream state – not fully awake. They decided it was best for him not to sleep on the top bunk because it was unsafe.

George was either sleep-walking or shouting out at least three times a week. During school holidays the problem seemed to get worse. He resisted bedtime and his parents still struggled to get him to bed before 9.30 pm. He woke at 7.15 am every morning, even at weekends, and, during the school holidays, he went to bed even later.

His parents were tired and frustrated by his night-time behaviour, especially as they both had stressful jobs. George seemed not to be affected and was surprised each morning to hear what he had done the previous night.

His parents tried limiting his intake of sweets and fizzy drinks, but the problem still continued. They also talked to him about anxieties - but he appeared to be happy at school and at home.

Diagnosis

George's night-time behaviour happened within 2–3 hours of him falling asleep, and he was unaware of his actions the next day. He was having night terrors and sleep-walking. He was also not getting enough sleep for his age, and therefore had a severe sleep deficit and was chronically tired. Sleep-deprived children have a greater need for deep sleep – and it is in this deep-sleep phase that sleep disturbances like George's occur.

Plan

The first aim was to ensure George had more sleep by getting him to bed earlier. This was done gradually by 15 minutes every fourth to seventh night, giving his body clock time to adjust. The speed at which the time was brought forward depended on how quickly George fell asleep. As George found it difficult to go to sleep, it was imperative that his bedtime routine was focused (lasting only 30–45 minutes), relaxing and calm. George's night-time disturbances were worse if he was over-stimulated in the day – especially just before bed – so his parents tried to avoid this, as well as sugary foods and drinks. A star chart was used to provide motivation.

Results

George was happy to go along with the new bedtime routine, as the time difference was very small initially and he was keen to get his reward. By the end of week 1, George's parents had managed to get him to sleep 30 minutes earlier. By day 5, George was sleeping through the night and had stopped having episodes of sleep-walking and night terrors.

From week 2 onwards, George was going to sleep 45 minutes earlier and bedtime was generally less stressful for the whole family. George was still earning stars, he seemed happier and his behaviour was calmer. He now had a set bedtime and his parents were advised to be consistent with this so that George's biological clock would become stable and regular so helping to prevent the reoccurrence of his sleep disturbances.

Steps

Use bathtime as a signal that bedtime is not far off.

Step 1 Introduce a quiet winding-down routine for your child, such as a snack of a banana and warm milk downstairs, then upstairs for a bath and into his bedroom for nightclothes, a story and lights out (see page 30, Creating a sleep routine).

Step 2 Introduce an earlier bedtime by bringing the time forward by 15 minutes every 3–7 nights. Check how much sleep is appropriate for your child's age and aim to get as close to it as possible. If your child has to wake for school make sure you set the bedtime to accommodate this.

Reward him for going to bed nicely with stars on a star chart (see page 83). Explain the star-chart system to your child, so that he understands why he is getting the stars, and negotiate his reward.

Step 3 Keep a sleep diary to monitor the time your child sleep-walks or has a night terror (see page 54, Sleep disturbances) then, for a week, wake him 15–30 minutes before his usual episode occurs. This has shown to be highly effective in preventing sleep disturbances.

When your child sleep-walks or has a night terror (see page 56), stay with him but don't try to wake him. Move any objects you think might hurt him, but let him go through the terror without intervention. He will then get back to sleep more quickly.

Depending on the size of the sleep deficit and your child's ability to go to sleep earlier, the programme will probably take 2–3 weeks to complete. Your child may resist the new bedtime, as he has in the past, and it may be several nights before you see any positive changes, but remain consistent – it will be worth it.

Solution 21 Getting up in the night

Try this plan if, like Jemima, your child gets up repeatedly after bedtime.

Problem

?

Jemima is 2½ years old, she has a 4-year-old sister. She had no apparent sleep problems until she developed an ear infection when she was 6 months old. After that, her parents found it difficult to settle her at bedtime and she would also wake during the night.

Jemima had a good bedtime routine: nightclothes, milk and a story in her room, brushing teeth, then lights out. This started at 6.00 pm and was over at 6.45 pm. Her parents said goodnight to her and went downstairs, they left her door ajar, with the landing light on. Jemima would then often get up and go downstairs several times. Each time she was taken back to bed and the tucking in ritual would be repeated. She would also often wake a couple of times in the night and go into her parents' room. After a cuddle and a sip of water, she would be taken back to bed. She would then sleep until 6.30–7.00 am.

Quote from mother *'Because we are tired we are more prone to arguments. We would like our daughter to sleep through the night without waking up. But we didn't want a technique that would take a long time or require our presence for long periods.'*

Diagnosis

Despite a good bedtime routine Jemima had problems going to sleep at bedtime and woke up during the night. Her parents were inadvertently rewarding Jemima's behaviour by cuddling, kissing and reassuring her each time she got out of her bed. While Jemima continued to receive these rewards she had no reason to change her behaviour and it had now become a habit.

Plan

To enable them to change this difficult night-time behaviour, her parents provided Jemima with clear and consistent boundaries. They removed the rewards for getting up and replaced them with a plan to ignore the unwanted behaviour (see page 77, Elimination). If she continued to get out of bed a door-shutting technique was used (see page 81), with clear boundaries and rewards from the sleep fairy for staying in bed.

Results

Jemima's behaviour changed quickly as she responded very well to the reward system. After 1 week of starting the programme, she was settling very well at bedtime without coming back downstairs, although her night waking got worse. Despite the clear bedtime boundaries, night waking had not been addressed: the parents were reluctant to start shutting the door for fear of Jemima's reaction.

The parents used the door-shutting technique for night waking from the beginning of week 2. They also changed the reward system. Jemima now had to stay in her bed all night for the sleep fairy to leave a reward. Initially Jemima stopped getting out of bed but yelled loudly until her parents responded. The reward system was extended even further to include no yelling. Jemima was so engaged with, and motivated by, the reward system that, by the end of week 2, she was sleeping through the night without getting up or yelling out.

Steps

Step 1 If your child is old enough, explain the new bedtime rules and what she has to achieve to get a reward. Be clear and concise with your explanation. Choose a bedtime for your child and stick to it, following a consistent, relaxing bedtime routine (see page 30, Creating a sleep routine). When tucking your child into bed, remind her of the conditions you have agreed together. Tell her that the sleep fairy will reward her if she does not get out of bed at bedtime (see page 82, Positive reinforcement – rewards).

Be realistic when setting goals you want your child to achieve – they can easily be adjusted as things progress.

Step 2 If your child gets out of bed, lead her back to bed but don't kiss and cuddle her. Resettle her and tell her that if she gets out of bed again you will have to come and shut the door. If she does get out of bed again you will have to use the door-shutting technique (see page 81).

Your child may become very distressed and angry. It may be necessary to hold the door shut until they get back into bed.

You can apply the door-shutting technique just as effectively with a stair gate.

Make sure the room is safe and that your child is not going to harm herself by climbing on furniture for example.

Step 3 Once your child is consistently achieving the agreed goal, carry on with your sleep fairy agreement in order to consolidate it. Even while you are maintaining the rewards, it is important to remember to praise her every morning when she achieves the desired sleep pattern. As you do this, you can gradually scale down and then stop the rewards (see page 83, Stopping the system).

Index

About Millpond

When Mandy Gurney and Tracey Marshall became mothers both were faced with children who wouldn't sleep. Suddenly having to cope with sleep problems themselves highlighted the lack of professional advice and support available for parents. 'There was nothing for it,' Mandy says, 'but to fall back on our years of working with children in the NHS and to do further study on the subject. We wanted to support parents in the same predicament and so set up an NHS sleep clinic. This was a great success and ran for five years, and made us realize we could use our expertise to help parents nationwide.' Thus Millpond was born. Since then their success rate in resolving children's sleep problems has been a staggering 97 per cent; they have become one of the country's leading authorities in this area and their highly successful techniques have featured in a number of television programmes. It's clear, they say, from the masses of satisfied parents that Millpond's system works; in fact 99 per cent of their clients have recommended them to their friends. 'This is why we encourage potential clients to read our testimonials and even speak to our clients direct to hear for themselves.'

If you would like to arrange a private consultation with Mandy or Tracey to support and guide you through your sleep programme email **enquiries@mill-pond.co.uk** or call 020 8444 0040. For more info visit **www.mill-pond.co.uk**

Don't hesitate; every day that goes by is a missed opportunity to get good night's sleep.

Acknowledgements

Thanks to all the families we have worked with over the years – their personal experiences gave us the inspiration to help other parents and write this book.

Thank you to Tessa Thomas for helping us to put our thoughts on to paper.

We would like to thank our families, especially our children, Alex, Lara, Rhese and Aidan, who are the reason we first became interested in solving sleep problems.

Last, to thank each other for support and understanding when times are tough.

Executive Editor Jane McIntosh
Editor Jessica Cowie
Executive Art Editor Rozelle Bentheim
Designer Mark Stevens
Production Controller Nigel Reed
Picture Research Sophie Delpech

Picture credits

Special Photography © Octopus Publishing Group Limited/Adrian Pope.
BananaStock 48, 68–69, 70, 89, 110–111, 117, 143.
Corbis UK Limited/Ariel Skelley 149;
/Jennie Woodcock 155.
Digital Vision 12-13, 22, 26, 52, 103, 112, 139, 147.
Getty Images/Altrendo Images 35;
/Clarissa Leahy 137; /James Muldowney 65;
/David Oliver 119; /Mel Yates 41.
Octopus Publishing Group Limited
/Peter Pugh-Cook 24, 57, 83, 113 top centre left, 125;
/Russell Sadur 29, 31, 38, 59, 60, 67, 74, 90–91, 93 top, 113 bottom centre left, 115, 127, 135, 141, 145.